CUTTING MORE
Ties That Bind

CUTTING MORE
Ties That Bind

Letting Go of Fear, Anger, Guilt, and Jealousy so We Can Educate Our Children and Change Ourselves

Phyllis Krystal

SAMUEL WEISER, INC.

York Beach, Maine

First published in the United States in 1993 by
Samuel Weiser, Inc.
Box 612
York Beach, Maine 03910

99 98 97 96 95 94 93
10 9 8 7 6 5 4 3 2 1

Library of Congress Cataloging-in-Publication Data
Krystal, Phyllis.
    Cutting more ties that bind : letting go of fear, anger, guilt, and
  jealousy so we can educate our children and change ourselves / by
  Phyllis Krystal.
        p. cm.
    Includes index.
    1. Visualization--Therapeutic use.   2. Psychotherapy.   3. Parent
  and child.   4. Autonomy (Psychology)   5. Symbolism (Psychology)
  6. Jung, C. G. (Carl Gustav), 1875-1961.   I. Title.
  RC489.F35K789   1993
  155.6'46--dc20   93-3964
                                                            CIP

ISBN 0-87728-792-9
BJ

Cover illustration is titled "Key Note."
Copyright © 1993 Richard Stodart. Used by kind permission.

Printed in the United States of America

The paper used in this publication meets the minimum requirements of
the American National Standard for Permanence of Paper for Printed
Library Materials Z39.48-1984.

I dedicate this book to Sri Sathya Sai Baba, whose life and teachings are an inspirational example of a true educator in every sense of the word.

CONTENTS

Preface   *ix*
Acknowledgments   *xiii*
Introduction   *xv*

Part 1

Chapter 1   Reprogramming and Preparation of Adults
            and Teachers   3
Chapter 2   Cutting Ties to Parents, and Other Techniques   7
Chapter 3   Sathya Sai Baba   12
Chapter 4   Preparing for Parenthood   19
Chapter 5   Bonding the Baby with the Parents   24
Chapter 6   The Birth Chart   28
Chapter 7   The Early Years: Pre-puberty   30
Chapter 8   Techniques for Use with Younger Children   36
Chapter 9   Puberty Rites   49
Chapter 10 Love   51
Chapter 11 Parental Control   54
Chapter 12 How Teachers Can Help   57
Chapter 13 Addictions   61

Part 2

Chapter 14 Who Are We and Why Are We Here?   67
Chapter 15 Early Conditioning   74
Chapter 16 Symbols   79
Chapter 17 Detaching Ourselves from Roles   83
Chapter 18 Men and Women   86

Chapter 19   Balloon and Nest-of-Dolls Roles   96
Chapter 20   The Effect of Roles on Future Relationships   106
Chapter 21   Identification with Occupation or Profession   113
Chapter 22   Inherited and Behavioural Patterns   116
Chapter 23   Sub-Personalities   121
Chapter 24   Freedom from Fear of Rejection   126
Chapter 25   Traditions, Customs and Mores   129
Chapter 26   Prejudices   131
Chapter 27   World Religions and their Effects   135
Chapter 28   Reincarnation and Karma   150
Chapter 29   Past Lives   158
Chapter 30   Dreams   176
Chapter 31   Thought and Thought-Forms   191

Index   199
About the Author   202

PREFACE

In the first book, readers are shown how to detach themselves from the more obvious outer security symbols or controlling factors in their lives, such as parents, teachers, family members, partners and friends, as well as material objects and aims such as money, jobs, cars, houses and various addictions.

But, after a person is free from these outer controls, there are many inner ones, to be released. These include inherited characteristics, character traits, familial behavioural patterns, religious and family affections, and a multitude of other influences to which we are heir as soon as we are born and take our place as members of a family.

After the first book had come out, specific techniques were forthcoming which clearly belonged in another book – this one.

Both my previous books had been started during visits to see Sathya Sai Baba in India. While staying at his ashram, I was able to concentrate for long uninterrupted periods, which is rarely the case during my very busy life at home, when my days are full, working with people individually, conducting seminars, answering the many letters and telephone calls requesting help, in addition to running a house and carrying out the duties of wife, mother, grandmother and friend. So, again, I decided to start the actual writing of this book on our next visit to Baba.

When we arrived in India, I discovered that the stage had already been set. Baba's very first question was, 'How is the new book and what is the title?' At that time I had given no thought to the choice of a title and was startled by the question which, from Baba's amused expression, was quite obviously his intention. I replied that it would probably be something like, *Cutting the Ties that Bind, Part Two*. On hearing this, he made a wry grimace and shook his head, indicating that he was not at all happy with that suggestion. He elaborated by saying, 'Swami does not like that at all.' So I quickly mentioned that my husband had chosen the titles for the first two books. Sidney replied that he could not provide a title until he had read the book, and it was only just being started. With that, Baba turned back to me with a questioning look, so I quickly asked him if he would supply the title. He smilingly agreed, saying, 'Swami will.' But how or when he would do so I had no idea. I was well aware that he would not necessarily tell me verbally, since he invariably discourages people from relying too heavily on his physical form or spoken word. Instead, he expects them to seek within, to receive their answers from the inner spark of divinity, what I have learned to call the High C. I, therefore, concentrated on writing the book and put the title out of my mind for the time being.

In addition to Baba's direct personal encouragement, I was given other very practical aids to allow me to concentrate on the task with minimal distractions. We had made an arrangement with an American couple to occupy our room at the ashram in our absence, which they had been doing since Baba's sixtieth birthday in November 1985. They had supervised tiling the floors to make it easier to clean in that very dusty place and the installation of netting at the open windows as protection from the voracious mosquitoes and other little creatures flying around in search of victims.

When we arrived, we were amazed and delighted with what greeted us. There were wooden frames to raise the mattresses from the floor, bookshelves and kitchen cabinets and even attractive curtains at the windows. It looked delightfully inviting. They had also arranged for a pleasant young Indian woman to cook for them and invited us to join them for the meals she prepared daily. So I was spared many of the usual time-consuming chores and could concentrate on writing. I daily gave thanks, both to Baba and to the American couple.

As I discovered when starting the other two books, when I was in Baba's physical presence, the ideas began to flow so fast and easily that I found it hard to put them into words and onto paper.

After a while I began to notice that though most of the subject matter followed the original theme, now and then what I found myself writing seemed to be irrelevant. I began to wonder if my mind could be playing tricks on me. As I continued to observe these seeming by-lanes along which it was straying, they started to fit together into a recognisable pattern. The common theme appeared to be a more successful education of children in contrast to the way most adults have been raised.

All of a sudden, as with the pieces of a jigsaw puzzle, everything fell into place and the words 'education' and 're-education' flashed into my mind. I immediately realised that not only had the title been given to me but the format of the book itself had been abruptly changed and expanded. Instead of the original theme I had conceived, the book would now be in two parts. The book that I had originally envisaged would now become Part 2. Part 1 would be new, and would include suggestions or guidelines to help parents and teachers to bring up children in such a way that each child would be encouraged to express his or her true nature with as little overlay from outer sources as possible. So the book would cover both education of children and re-education of adults who had not had the advantage of being taught in such an enlightened way.

The next time I saw Baba, I volunteered that I thought he had given me a better title for the book and told him what had come to my mind. He smiled broadly and said, 'Yes, Swami likes that much better.' Of course! I now understood that the whole theme fits perfectly into Baba's mission of concentrating primarily on presenting a more complete and satisfactory method of education than now exists throughout the world. He says that the world will change for the better only if the children of today are taught to live according to basic human values, particularly love. Then, when they mature and take their places in the many diverse institutions in their own countries, they will be prepared to put into practice the moral training they have been given in addition to the regular academic knowledge. Baba often points out that most adults have become too set in their ways and fixed in their attitudes to be capable of much change, whereas children and young people are more malleable and open to direction.

I had considered the original theme to be quite intimidating in its scope. Now, with this unexpected addition, it was positively overwhelming. However, a comforting thought quickly presented itself. How could I forget, even for a minute, that I, as an individual ego, would not be writing this book any more than I had the other two? By seeking contact with the High C, I would, as before, receive it piece by piece from the source. In doing so, I would be gaining further practice in relying solely on that wise, loving and real part of myself.

However, this method of writing can be most disconcerting at times. Since it is not controlled by the ego, patience needs to be cultivated when the natural flow stops and appears to have dried up, often for extended periods. I have gradually learned to sense when the time is right and avoid trying to use force when it no longer flows easily. In retrospect, I always see how perfect the timing has been whenever I surrender my personal ego to the High C and trust it to direct me when the time is right and accept whenever that may be. But this attitude is in direct opposition to all that most people have been taught, and old habits die hard.

During our stay at the ashram, Baba frequently inquired how the book was progressing and from time to time made remarks which showed me that he was silently supervising it.

At our farewell interview, I handed him the sheaf of pages I had by then written in my illegible handwriting that he had once referred to as crow's feet scratches. As he riffled through the pages, I asked if it was the way he wished it to be. He turned quickly away from scanning the sheets and with his extraordinary eyes penetrating to my very depths, said, 'No, that is incorrect. Is it the way *you* think it should be?' He stressed the word 'you', as he pointed his forefinger at me and looked deep into my soul. Again, he was reminding me that I must learn to rely, not on him personally, but on my real Self deep within me. As his eyes pierced the shell of my body, mind and emotions, I experienced an intense understanding that this inner Self is the only part he really sees. It is as if he bypasses our frail and faulty personalities in order to make contact with our real Self. His message to me was that I must constantly turn within to consult It and allow It to guide me. Baba's human form, living in India, is here to remind all who will listen that this inner teacher to which we all have access, whenever we seek It within instead of outside ourselves, is our true Self.

Many times since then, while writing, I have vividly recalled his gaze and, turning within, have asked for direction and waited for thoughts to enter my mind after I have emptied it of its flurry of worries, questions and doubts. With practice it becomes easier to make this drastic change away from the way we have all been taught to seek our answers and security from external experiences, from books and other people.

ACKNOWLEDGMENTS

I would like to thank, first and foremost, the High C, the unchanging Reality, resident within all, for help in supplying the various techniques and symbols whenever I or others have requested help. This, of course, to me includes Sathya Sai Baba who symbolises the High C in human form.

Secondly, I thank all the individuals and groups who have diligently used the symbols and have thus imbued them with power.

I also thank those who have been willing to give their time and energy to join me, and other partners, on the Triangle to seek help for the many who, for various reasons, were unable to participate in person. One of these helpers is my daughter, Sheila, who in addition offered to take on the heroic task of painstakingly editing this manuscript. It is an invaluable help since she uses the work in her practice as a psychologist and, therefore, she is well placed to determine whether the text is accurate and clearly explained.

I also owe a very big debt of gratitude to Peggy Lenney for so generously offering to type the many drafts of the manuscript until, at last, it was complete.

And, lastly, I thank my husband Sidney for his continued support and helpful suggestions.

INTRODUCTION

In my first book, *Cutting the Ties That Bind*, I set forth a method of counselling based on the understanding that our true identity is not, as many people believe, the temporary and imperfect body or the personality. It is much more than that. It is the inner, permanent and perfect Self which I refer to as the High C – the Higher Consciousness. Most people are unaware of It because It is hidden from sight, unlike the outer physical form.

The method given in this book is designed to help individuals make contact with this inner reality and allow It to guide them in their daily lives as only It is wise enough to do.

The techniques and symbols employed can help those who choose to use them to cut the ties to any controlling factors which prevent them from following the directions of their High C. These include people, things, desires and beliefs and thought-systems that have control over them.

We cannot serve two masters, nor can we be guided solely by the High C, our one reliable inner mentor, until the distraction or control by all the other security symbols is removed. Only then can we know who we really are and be at peace.

Since this method was first defined, there have been many new developments.

I have been working more extensively with children and teenagers and, in the process, it has become apparent that the work can be very helpful in raising and educating children. But so that this system can be successfully used with them, it is necessary for parents and other adults concerned with their training to experience the work themselves and then to be willing to use it in their own lives in order to enable them to introduce it to children.

Accordingly, this book is divided into two parts. The first contains methods of applying the work to children, together with suggestions for understanding and using it by parents and others responsible for their training. Included in this part are certain teachings of Sathya Sai Baba that supplement and implement the work.

The second part presents new insights and more advanced techniques. It gives instructions on how to release oneself from the larger, multiple, more complex systems that have programmed our behaviour in specific ways. These include the familial and national customs, religious and political affiliations, the various roles people play, the hats they wear, superstitions and taboos, prejudices and fears, and a host of other influences to which we are all heir as soon as we are born and again as we take our places as members of a family. This part also includes material on reincarnation and dream interpretation.

It ends with a brief summary of the most recent work on negative thought-forms. We have all contributed some energy to these, by our negative thoughts, in this as in past lives. Also considered are various addictions, with the powerful thought-forms to which they are attached; it is these forces that control the addicts, and that is why it is so hard to break away from such compulsions.

This book, like the first two, is the result of learning to consult the inner guide within everyone whether or not we are aware of it. I shall be referring to this inner reservoir of wisdom and love as the High C, or Higher Consciousness, as I did in my first book on the subject. With practice, we can succeed in breaking with the old ways in which we have all been taught to seek answers and security from outer influences, such as people, books and various thought-systems, and to arrive at this very different but more effective way of finding the answers within ourselves.

CUTTING MORE
Ties That Bind

PART 1

Chapter 1

REPROGRAMMING AND PREPARATION OF ADULTS AND TEACHERS

Surely, the first requisite for a more successful system of educating children is the re-education of adults, precisely because children are, of necessity, trained by adults, both parents and teachers. Consequently, adults need to be re-educated in a manner very different from their own original indoctrination.

The chain-reaction that can be observed in patterns of behaviour handed down from one generation to the next must be broken. This will allow human beings to develop into self-reliant, independent, mature men and women, free to make choices between what is currently appropriate and the often outmoded or negative patterns handed down to them through their family heritage. These old patterns can be so constricting that change and progress become impossible for those imprisoned by them. We so often mechanically and unthinkingly echo whatever we have heard all our lives without even questioning whether it is true or useful in day-to-day life. Many people live through an entire lifetime automatically following inherited patterns of behaviour whether they are currently practical or not.

All the more primitive species learn by the repetition of tried and proven behaviour, either as directly taught by their parents or as copied from them. In this way it is imprinted on their nervous systems and acts as a defence against attack, hunger and other problems they may encounter. It allows them instinctively to know how and when to react.

But, though human beings are like animals in many ways, they do not live solely on the instinctive plane. They possess the abilities of thinking, reasoning, questioning and being creative in many ways in addition to eating, sleeping and producing offspring. Therefore, they are able individually to form new habits to fit changing times and conditions.

In the last fifty years there have been more drastic changes than in any comparable period in history. These changes have provided many advantages, but at the same time they have also created more problems. Such has been the pace of change that we have been forced to make many huge adjustments in a very short space of time. The result is a great deal of general confusion and insecurity.

At present there exists throughout the world an acute need to reshape the systems of education in order to give children growing up in this rapidly changing scene some very necessary new guidelines. These could replace those that are either totally missing or are so outmoded that they are of little practical use in present-day society. This situation has caused disorder, licence, depravity, addiction to drugs, alcoholism, sexual confusion, violence, delinquency and depression, often leading to youthful suicides.

When the essential meaning of life is no longer taught, either verbally or through example, our children grow up in a seemingly senseless but sense-dominated world that provides no emotional or spiritual sustenance. They then begin to crave they know not what. To satisfy this inner hunger, they turn desperately to anyone or anything that holds out even the slightest promise of assuaging it. Hence, the proliferation of multi-sexual encounters, the enormously increased reliance on drugs, alcohol, violent films and television shows, salacious books and magazines and even certain forms of 'pop' meditation. All these either overstimulate them, and in that way distract them from their pain and hunger, or dull their perceptions by numbing uncomfortable thoughts and feelings.

This part will, therefore, be a summary or overview of my first book. It will prepare parents and teachers by first showing them how to free themselves of the old negative conditioning and to avoid passing it on to the children under their care.

Many people will resist this idea as being highly impractical, citing the old saw, 'You can't teach an old dog new tricks.' But humans are not animals, though they do share many attributes. They have many advantages over other species, the most important one being free will. They are therefore not obliged to continue outmoded habits. Changing them may involve a great deal of hard work, but with determination, and the help of the High C, it is most certainly possible.

They will then be in a better position to bring children up in such a way that their innate abilities and personalities are allowed to flower, instead of being masked by the ideas of their educators.

Obviously, parents and teachers and all other figures of authority in a child's life need to be acutely aware of their very important roles in teaching and programming the children with whom they are closely associated. Only by training children, the future citizens of each country, is it possible for a change of consciousness to be brought about in the world, composed as it is of countries, organisations and families all containing individuals.

Only when adults sincerely try to apply to their own personal lives the time-tested human values comprising the world-wide and many-faceted heritage outlined in the various ancient teachings can they become capable of teaching them to the children who come under their influence.

By ancient teachings, I refer to the original truth received by inspired teachers, sages and seers through the ages. This truth has been lost to sight beneath the accretion of man-made embellishments. Regrettably, it is the latter on which the various disciplines have been built. But they are now fast crumbling or are already lost. This is as it should be if the original truth is to be reclaimed and presented in a form more appropriate to the times. The Shiva (or Destroyer) energy is at work, whereby old rigidified guidelines are being demolished in many areas to make room for new growth to break through. It is similar to the way a field must be ploughed before fresh seeds can be planted to produce a new crop.

At present we are all living in an interim period, watching the rapid demolition of many old and familiar patterns to which we have become so accustomed that they represent security. As yet there are no clear indications of the kinds of new patterns which might eventually replace them.

Very few people are comfortable in unfamiliar situations. These can be most anxiety-producing to some for the simple reason that they may not have had the experience to help themselves to handle them. No one likes to feel at a loss or inadequate. For those who are aware of the current changes taking place everywhere, these are very difficult and frequently bewildering times in which to be alive.

All species feel more comfortable with parameters or guidelines, even if some individuals may often wish to discard them and live free of restraint. Invariably, such rebellion ends in disaster, just as a runaway vehicle lacking control or direction eventually crashes.

First, before anyone can be taught new patterns of behaviour, the old and inappropriate ones must be relinquished. For this reason, I always suggest to couples who are planning to start a family that they work through some of the techniques from my first book before they embark on their new joint venture of parenthood.

First, the clearly observable chain-reaction proceeding from one generation to the next must be broken so that each new generation is free from any of the old negative conditioning that so often prevents growth. It is very simply expressed by the biblical quotation, 'The sins of the fathers shall be visited upon the children to the third and fourth generation.' Children react to parents either by copying them or rebelling against their identity, and how they behave and what they teach. But both such reactions inhibit their ability to express themselves freely and, consequently, restrict their development (or restrain their full development).

It is therefore imperative for prospective parents to cut the binding ties to each of their own parents, surrogate parents, or other authority figures. They themselves must be free to make contact with the High C and to henceforth receive instruction and direction from that inner source instead of from outer ones associated with their own hopes and fears, habits and objectives.

Chapter 2

CUTTING
TIES TO PARENTS,
AND OTHER TECHNIQUES

The first step before cutting the ties to parents is to prevent intrusion, control or coercion from any outer sources by delineating and protecting one's inner space or territory. This is accomplished by using the Figure Eight (described in *Cutting the Ties that Bind*). A person is directed to visualise, think of, or imagine on the ground all around him a golden circle with a radius the length of his arm with the fingers extended. This circle sets the limits of the holy ground or *temenos*, as the Greeks named it, space or territory, to use current terms. If the person is more than usually vulnerable, this circle can be imagined extending upward to form a cylinder all around him as high as feels comfortable and protective. Another golden circle about the same size, and containing one of the parents, is imagined on the ground immediately in front of him, the two circles just touching without overlapping. It will be easily seen that the Figure Eight has been formed. However, the two circles alone do not prevent intrusion or projection by either person into the other's territory. To free both from invasion or control by the other, a neon blue light is visualised, imagined or actually drawn on paper, starting at the point where the two circles touch. It flows first around the parent's circle in a clockwise direction, and back to where they touch. It continues around the person's left side, around his back to his right side, and back again to where they touch. It then flows around the Figure Eight continuously. The neon blue light has the effect of drawing each person's projections into his or her own circle, rather like disentangling the tentacles of two octopuses entwined in each other's grasp.

This visualisation needs to be practised daily for two minutes upon awakening, again just before going to sleep and at intervals during the day, for two weeks. The actual exercise for severing the tight constricting ties between the two people can then be undertaken. Briefly, it involves visualising or feeling one or more bonds connecting the person and his parents, and mentally removing and destroying them in whatever way is indicated by the High C. The next step involves a ritual in which the person thanks the parent for all the learning gained from the relationship, asks the parent for forgiveness for any wrongs perpetrated against him or her and requests the High C to forgive him or her for any wrongs against himself for which the parent has been responsible. The parent is then asked to leave the inner space, which allows more direct contact with the High C, the only true authority. A ritual bath to remove all overlay of the parent's attitudes completes the ritual.

Separate rituals should be undertaken for each parent and any other individuals responsible for early conditioning or programming. This method successfully frees a person from the overlay of old patterns learned from the parents during childhood which do not necessarily allow expression of the real personality.

After the cutting ritual, it is helpful to compile two lists, one for each parent, setting forth the positive and negative attributes of each. These help to determine where he has copied and where he has rebelled against the model of conduct they have presented to him. Unless these qualities are clearly seen, it is difficult for a person to decide where any correction of habits, attitudes or other learned characteristics is needed in his own behaviour. Only when they have freed themselves in this way are prospective parents able to rear their own children more effectively by helping them to reveal their true personalities instead of projecting on to them their own hopes, ideals, expectations, preferences and other inherited patterns as so many parents usually do.

Unlike animals, human beings have free will and have the right to decide for themselves whether to follow a slow evolutionary path or to work to eradicate their faults and weaknesses. They can then detach themselves from past mistakes and be free to start living more positively in the present under the guidance of the High C.

Many other exercises outlined in the previous book would greatly aid prospective parents in preparing for their own children. I will merely refer to each of them here and suggest that the reader study these steps, described in the first book.

The Tree

The Tree technique, whereby prospective parents make contact with their own version of the inner Cosmic Parents, which together form the High C, is most helpful. So many people have had unhappy relationships with one or both parents and find the discovery of their own inner ones a tremendous comfort and support. Many people have never received love in a form they can accept and have not been taught either how to give love or how to receive it, simply because the parents themselves were not given loving role models by their parents. When they make contact with these loving inner parents they find they can receive from them the love that they had always longed for. They can then allow it to flow through them to other people.

Negative Emotions

The various techniques for detaching oneself from negative emotions such as fear, anger, guilt, jealousy and envy, to name just a few, are an excellent preparation for assuming the responsibility of rearing children, who frequently stir up all manner of unpleasant reactions in parents unless they have released these feelings beforehand. Often parents will vent their anger on their children over some trifling incident. Their child often has no idea how he has evoked such an exaggerated outburst.

The Inner House

Working with the Inner House and setting it in order is another very helpful undertaking, since the house is a symbol of the entire self with the various rooms representing all its parts. The actual house in which they live can also be cleaned and put in order at the same time, which greatly emphasises the message to the subconscious.

The Inner Child

Identifying the Inner Child, attending to its needs and giving it love and attention to help that part of the personality to grow to the same age as the rest of the personality is extremely important. Otherwise, there is apt to be a conflict between the Inner Child of each parent and the outer physical child they bring into their lives.

The Black Cloud

If a Black Cloud is suspected as a negative influence on either of the parents' families, it should by all means be dissipated before a child is born into a family. These negative inherited memories can be triggered at any time if one of the members of a family faces a situation that is reminiscent of old family traumas.

The above techniques or exercises are recommended as indispensable for prospective parents. However, it would of course be very helpful if they would both go through the rest of the exercises described in *Cutting the Ties that Bind* to remove anything else that could cause problems while their children are growing up.

We all feel more secure when we have clear guidelines to direct us in our daily lives. That is one reason why some old customs continue to be followed despite the fact that many of them have either degenerated into senseless rules or are no longer relevant to life at the present time.

Children tend to learn more easily and quickly by example than by words. If parents live according to high moral standards, their children are more likely to follow their lead. If, on the other hand, the parents teach one thing but do another, children are quick to detect the inconsistency and become confused.

During my childhood in England, I was quoted as repeatedly having said to my mother from a very early age, 'You tell me not to lie, but you do it all the time. That's not fair.' This reaction is typical of young children before they have become too inhibited to express themselves freely. It is very easy to teach others but that is not enough. Children need to be shown by the example of elders and teachers the type of behaviour and practices which match their teachings. Not all teachers have high standards, so discrimination is needed to distinguish between those who only teach the truth and those who also practise it.

Chapter 3

SATHYA
SAI BABA

Many years after I first started to receive the counselling method I use, I heard about Sathya Sai Baba, a world teacher who lives in Southern India. He was born in 1926 in a tiny remote village and has been quietly and patiently teaching all those who are willing to listen to his message which, like that of Jesus and other spiritual teachers of the past, is based on unselfish love.

Since 1972, when I first heard about Baba, I have visited him many times in India and have been able to watch him in many different situations and with thousands of people.

No ordinary human being could do even a fraction of what he accomplishes every single day, year after year. Each day's activities represent a superhuman feat which I doubt anyone could match. And he accomplishes it all with such unhurried, unruffled serenity and, above all, with immense love. Sai Baba's life is his message, as he often avers. I have certainly found this to be true. Experiencing Sai Baba's influence is a challenge to bring our lives into line with his teachings. In so doing, we can give a clear example to others who may be in need of guidance.

Sai Baba, in his wisdom, knows that we all need to be taught carefully and clearly, one step at a time, like children. So he has initiated several different programmes to help all those who wish to advance, each at his own pace, and bring their lives in line with his teachings.

Particularly at present there is an acute need for ground rules or a model upon which we can mould our lives. This could help to provide a clearer picture of how far short we fall from the model we have chosen to follow. For how can we sense when our lives and behaviour are out of line unless we have a well-defined outline to follow which we know really works?

From my personal experience, as well as that of many with whom I have worked individually and in groups, Sai Baba's few simple and clear programmes have proved to be an excellent and workable system. They can help all those who so desire to work on themselves. Eventually, they will discover who they really are beneath the many coverings of habits, desires and roles which hide their real self not only from their own view, but also from the eyes of others.

So I shall use Sai Baba's models first to illustrate how people can conduct their own lives and, secondly, how to train their children. However, I do not wish to convey the impression that Baba's is the only way. It is important, in fact imperative, to choose a model that really works, and continue to use it until the results are experienced. I will keep my presentation of Baba's teachings as brief as possible. If more details are desired, there are many books devoted entirely to his teachings taken from his numerous discourses, as well as many others written by devotees citing their own experiences.

Essentially, Baba teaches that love is the most important and effective force in the universe. One of his oft-quoted sayings illustrates this point: 'Start the day with love, spend the day with love, fill the day with love, end the day with love. That is the way to God.' Now that sounds wonderful and we are all inclined to agree, but do we practise it, even occasionally during the day, let alone all day? We argue that we are too busy, that life is too hectic, that we forget. These are excuses. If we could practise it even a small part of the time, now and then, we would begin to observe that our lives gradually, almost imperceptibly, do become calmer and less rushed. We would also find we had time for much more than we ever dreamed possible.

Baba further advises that we should undertake everything we do as an act of worship. That means that when we are faced with an unpleasant or menial task we should do it as an offering to the universal God-force. Likewise, when the occasion arises to serve another person, instead of doing so with a subservient attitude, a patronising one, or feeling resentful or put-upon, we should consider the other person as a manifestation of God. This is true even though it is often buried out of sight behind an unpleasant personality.

Baba does not advocate the exclusive use of routines and rituals in our present period of history. He recommends that, instead of rigidly adhering to a fixed programme of meditation, prayer and other practices, we should endeavour to live the entire day as a continuous meditation. Baba materialised for me a *japamālā* which is like a rosary. It is composed of 108 crystal beads. When I asked him if I should use a mantra with it for meditation, he said, 'No, it must be continuous meditation all day.'

Education in Human Values

Baba's Education in Human Values (EHV) programme can be very helpful for parents and teachers as well as for children of all ages. In preparing for parenthood, it can be used to help both parents to compare their life-style with this model. The basic tenets are Truth, Right Action, Peace, Love and Non-Violence. The list may be rather intimidating at first glance. However, when it is broken down in detail, it proves to be a most practical and positive method for guiding both children and adults towards a more fulfilling way of life.

Naturally, parents and teachers will find that they are not able to put all these values into practice immediately. It takes time to weed out old negative habits, attitudes, thoughts and feelings to make room for more positive ones to take their place. Only one small step at a time should be attempted, otherwise the prospect of such a colossal task can become overwhelming.

In my counselling work, I use a method which has proved to be very helpful in clarifying the steps. I suggest to the person with whom I am working that he purchase a package of multi-coloured postcards or paper. He can designate a card of a chosen colour to represent each of the five tenets. For instance, a pink card could be for love, a white card for truth, blue for peace, yellow for right action, and green for non-violence.

It is advisable to allow one week at a time to work on each value. After that they can be repeated as often as required. Daily incidents that indicate whether the particular value has been adhered to, or the reverse, can be recorded on the applicable card each day. This record gives a very clear picture of how far a person is succeeding in applying these principles to daily life. Merely reading or hearing about such a programme is not enough. It is necessary to *apply it* and experience it in action to bring about the necessary changes in oneself in the context of everyday life. Only then are the teachings absorbed on many levels and not solely by the mind.

Truth

So, in the first week, Truth could be the subject under scrutiny. If the adults responsible for teaching children are not adhering to truth in their lives, how can they expect the children to learn to be truthful? There are many different aspects to truth besides the obvious one of honesty or telling the truth. Thoughts, attitudes and actions need to be checked against this value, as well as words. So, thought, word *and* deed must be integrated and based in Truth.

Right Action

It is difficult to find one word to give a precise interpretation of the Sanskrit word *dharma*, but the nearest equivalent in English is probably Right Action. It literally means the intrinsic nature of a person or thing, that which makes it what it is, its essential essence or aroma, its 'isness'. A bell has a tone, a flower a perfume, a fruit a taste which is its own. A pomegranate cannot taste like an apple. Likewise, a man's *dharma* cannot be the same as a dog's, a butterfly's or an oak's *dharma*. Nor can one man's specific duty be the same as another man's.

Everyone and everything in the world contains a spark of divinity clothed or housed in a certain tangible form through which it can be manifested. It is similar to electricity, which needs to be harnessed to, or directed through, different appliances or avenues to create certain effects. It can heat through a fire, a heating pad or an oven; cool through a freezer, a fan or an air-conditioning system, and so on. The universal God-force is manifested in the world through the multitudes of things, minerals, plants, animals and human beings.

People need to make an effort to allow this force to be expressed in their lives since they alone possess the free will to make that choice. In other words, it means surrendering to the High C their true identity and obeying Its subtle directions instead of allowing the five senses, with their myriad attachments and desires, to control their lives.

So, when we understand and start to live according to Right Action, or are inwardly directed by the High C, we will find that we are in the right place, at the right time, engaged in the right activity, for the right reason or motive.

Actually, the only way Right Action can be successfully incorporated into our lives is by daily asking the High C to express Itself through us. That will circumvent the habitual ego-motivated way of life so apparent in the world today.

I have found it helpful to start each day by asking in meditation for the High C to think, speak, feel and act through me and to remember to use as a mantra, 'Surrender, Trust and Accept', throughout the day. This daily practice helps me to bring about Right Action in my life.

When we have begun to understand Truth, Right Action will naturally follow and when they have become habitual, peace, love and non-violence will naturally be incorporated into our lives.

Peace

Being at peace results from High C-directed living. When we relax and allow the High C to take over, we will not be plagued by the previous swarms of doubts and indecisions and the proliferation of desires which cause so much stress and unrest. In today's world, television and advertising in the media constantly lure us to seek peace in possessions and activities rather than from within ourselves. Eventually, we discover that we are left with the opposite of peace as we search frantically for what we hope will give it to us.

Love

When we are really trying to be motivated by the High C, instead of our egos, we will be more and more in touch with our Reality. As Its very nature is Love, it will be quite natural to begin to express Love in thought, word and deed.

To quote Baba, 'Love as thought is Truth. Love as action is Right Action. Love as feeling is Peace. Love as understanding is non-violence or harmlessness.'

Non-Violence

Non-violence means doing nothing consciously to hurt or harm anyone in any way by thought, word or deed. But non-violence has a much wider meaning than is generally recognised. Not only are vegetarianism and the majestic turning of the other cheek non-violence, but so are the care and concern we express for our planet and its life-forms.

Ceiling on Desires

A further help to prospective parents in reorganising their life-style before inviting other souls to share it is Sai Baba's Ceiling on Desires programme. It is designed to reduce waste in four different categories: money, food, time and energy.

This programme was offered by Baba to ensure that families could benefit to the optimum from the various resources at their disposal. When any of these are wasted, the family suffers a reduced standard of living.

- Unless the available money is put to good use, the family will not be assured of basic necessities.

- If food is wasted or does not provide adequate nourishment, the family will not be strong and healthy.

- If time is frittered away on wasteful activities, the children will suffer from lack of parental attention they need to assure them of their own worth.

- Similarly, if the parents waste their energy in indulging in emotions such as fear, anger, envy and jealousy, or debilitate themselves by becoming addicted to such things as alcohol, drugs, cigarettes, gambling or any of the host of other destructive habits, they will have too little energy to devote to their children's needs and, equally important, in enjoying healthy family pursuits with them.

A booklet compiled from devotees' suggestions is available to help those who are interested in using this programme. It is entitled, *Suggestions for Study Groups and Individual Use of the Ceiling on Desires Programme*. It is available from the Sri Sathya Sai Baba Book Center of America, PO Box 278, Tustin, California 92780.

Chapter 4

PREPARING
FOR PARENTHOOD

The education of a child actually starts before birth, so prospective
parents should ask themselves what their real motives are for
wanting children of their own. Obviously, I am referring neither
to the many supposedly accidental pregnancies nor the unwanted
ones. Too few young people anticipating becoming parents do so
with pure motives. Many are pushed into parenthood almost in
spite of themselves, instead of voluntarily, by family pressure to
follow the accepted or conventional pattern. Often their own
parents' intense desire to have grandchildren will lead a couple
to comply, if only to avoid feeling guilty.

Some people elect to have a baby to repair a shaky relationship.
Others want to have someone to love, or to give them the love they
are not receiving from their partner.

Many families desire an heir to their fortune or estate, a successor
to the father after he retires or dies. Others want to have children to
care for them in their old age. This expectation often prevents the
children from living their own lives.

All the above and many other motives are selfish, with little
consideration for the welfare of the person entering the family.
The conscious decision by a couple to become parents allows a
soul the opportunity to incarnate. It can then learn whatever it still

needs to experience as well as expend the energy contained in old negative thoughts and actions from past lives. Couples who think primarily in terms of a tiny baby when considering having a child should realise that it will not remain a baby indefinitely. It bears within it a seed ready to germinate and blossom into an individual person under their care.

Sai Baba teaches that a human birth is a great privilege. In that case, it is also a great privilege to be the parents who make it possible and that should therefore be the primary motive for undertaking such an immense responsibility.

Preparation for the Birth of a Child

There is an ancient theory that a soul about to re-enter the earth scene is magnetically attracted to a developing embryo formed by the union of specific parents in an environment best suited to its needs for working out its past karma.

It could, therefore, be concluded that prospective parents can, to a certain extent, influence the type of child they will attract by their characters, attitudes, life-style and motives for becoming parents. Consequently, a relatively serious approach is preferable to the haphazard way many people enter parenthood.

Undertaking the responsibility of rearing and guiding a child needs careful preparation. Since the child will be drawn to a suitable situation for its learning, the parents should make their environment as harmonious as possible. By that, I do not refer merely to the material factors of wealth, position and physical benefits, but rather to the attitude of welcome and the promise of loving care that assures the child of the security it needs during infancy and childhood.

Many couples with whom I have worked have made very careful preparations for the arrival of their children. Some of them accept this new responsibility as an opportunity to examine themselves, their relationship with one another and their combined lives, and attempt to bring all the factors closer to an ideal situation for the entry of a child.

Some couples pray for guidance in preparing for the arrival of the expected child and ask for dreams or other signs to help them. During the pregnancy, some elect to start a daily routine of speaking to the foetus, assuring it that they really want to be its parents and adding an extremely important reassurance, namely, that they would welcome either a boy or a girl. I am always delighted when parents have no preference. I still vividly remember when I was in the hospital following the birth of each of my daughters, hearing screams issuing from a nearby room. Each time I asked the reason, I was told that the mother was very disappointed with the sex of her baby and did not want to accept it. I was horrified at the time and wondered what effect this immediate rejection would have on the child. Since then, I have learned from some of the people with whom I have worked just what a negative effect such a rejection did have on their entire lives.

To desire a child of the preferred sex is in direct opposition to the principle of 'Thy will, not mine'. It is ego-inspired instead of High C-directed and it prevents union with the God-Self. Thus the indwelling soul of the parent regresses instead of evolving.

There are other very important conditions to be considered preparatory to the birth of a baby to ensure that it will be given a good start in life. These include the health and habits of both parents, but especially those of the mother-to-be. Many warnings are now being given by doctors concerning the deleterious effects on a developing embryo of drugs, tobacco, alcohol and many other items that common sense should recognise as injurious to a developing embryo entirely dependent on the mother's body, absorbing whatever she ingests.

Many articles, films and videos are being produced to alert people to the especially disastrous effects of drugs. For instance, a child born to parents who habitually use heroin, cocaine or other addictive drugs is likely to be born addicted. It is heart-rending to see newborn babies suffering from withdrawal symptoms, let alone the more serious problems they are heir to.

In all cultures there are so-called old wives' tales influencing what should or should not be done during pregnancy. Some of these are based on truth and should be adhered to, while others have grown out of old superstitions no longer valid. Good common sense is the best guide. But there is no excuse for neglecting to search for current information based on scientific experiments; it is usually easily obtainable from local libraries. There are also helpful prenatal classes for both parents which can allay many of the fears caused by lack of precise knowledge.

Many women elect to have their children by natural childbirth methods. Classes are now being offered which both parents can attend in preparation for such a birth. These are an invaluable aid, especially during a first pregnancy. There is nothing more helpful than both parents being as prepared as possible for the forthcoming event. It is also very encouraging for both parents to participate in the choice of a doctor or midwife. Fortunately, many doctors now co-operate with those who prefer natural childbirth. Some also specialise in innovative ways of tending the newborn baby, by prescribing warm baths, oil rubs and gentle massage to ease the first few minutes of life outside the security and comfort of the mother's womb. In Britain, it is now common practice for hospitals to allow the mother to have her baby nearby in a cot to make the initial separation less traumatic for them both.

There are many excellent books and films available presenting various new methods of tending the baby immediately following its birth. Drs Le Boyer and Lamaze were two of the foremost innovators along these lines. Their books, as well as others, are readily procurable from local libraries. Video films can also be purchased or rented well in advance of the time when such information will be needed. These help to prepare the parents by answering many of their questions as they approach the time for delivery and will ensure a calm mind, their fears allayed.

Choosing a Midwife or Doctor

The choice of doctor or midwife is very important. Since the relationship with him or her will continue for at least nine months, it is most desirable that it be harmonious. This is especially important for the expectant mother, to ensure that she will feel free to discuss any worrying symptoms or fears and ask any questions that may arise.

Pregnancy can be a stressful time, especially the first time it is experienced. Every woman should have the right to select a doctor or midwife with whom she feels comfortable and secure and whom she senses will be supportive of her and help to reduce stress as much as possible. Some people hesitate to change doctors when, on closer acquaintance with the one they first chose, they discover an incompatibility or a lack of confidence and ease. If that is so, a woman should seek another more to her liking. The briefly unpleasant task of terminating the relationship with the first one is a small price to pay for the increased comfort and relaxation of the ensuing months. Changing doctors is not a punishable offence, and an expectant mother owes is not only to herself but to the developing baby, her husband and any other members of her family who could be affected by her own uneasiness.

Chapter 5

BONDING THE BABY WITH THE PARENTS

The very first rite is that of bonding the new baby to each of its parents. In the first twenty minutes after birth, a baby can focus its eyes. Another reason why natural childbirth is preferable to other methods involving the use of anaesthesia is that both mother and child are fully conscious. The bonding takes place when the baby is held so that it can look directly into the eyes of each parent. This contact is very important as it gives the baby a sense of security and belonging in the unfamiliar new world it has just entered from the safety and warmth of its mother's womb.

In addition to the eye contact, the baby needs to be reassured of its welcome into the family. This can be accomplished both verbally and through warm physical contact, such as holding and caressing, to ensure that it starts its new life with a sense of security, something all babies must be given. The experience of being welcomed and loved sets the stage for it to develop normally, without the feeling of rejection that so many children have and later come to expect from all others for the rest their lives, frequently with tragic results.

Naming a Child

The naming of a child is another very important ceremony. It gives it an identity for the rest of its life. Like most other rituals, this too has lost much of its deeper significance and in many cases is omitted altogether. Invariably, the parents decide on names for their child some time during the pregnancy, as soon as they can agree on appropriate ones for either sex. The names are then included on the birth certificate and that, in many instances, is the end of the matter.

The old rituals held more meaning. Names were considered very important in distinguishing a child from others in the family and ensuring its rights as an individual. In some cultures, names are chosen according to custom. In India, for instance, children are often named after a god, either as a blessing or to represent a special virtue or attribute it is hoped the child will develop as it matures. More often in the past than now, Christian families chose names like Patience, Hope or Constance to encourage children to develop such virtues. Similarly, the names of famous figures from history or myth are sometimes chosen, in the hope that the child might emulate them. In the Jewish culture, children are often named after a deceased relative or biblical figure, but rarely after living people. In other cultures, children are frequently given the names of living relatives, especially those of the mother or father, hence the many 'juniors' to distinguish sons from their fathers. However, a name can be a heavy burden if a child is expected to live up to the fame, success or brilliance of a namesake.

Before they settle on a name for their child, it would be an excellent idea if the parents would think ahead and try to determine the possible effect the various names under consideration might have on the child as it grows to adulthood, and to consider, too, the possible effect of shortened versions that might be used. It is a well-known fact that children can be, and often are, very cruel to one another. A child's name can cause a great deal of unnecessary misery if it makes him the butt of his peers' ridicule.

Pet names, nicknames and those variations on the original name initiated by younger siblings while trying and failing to pronounce the whole name but producing their own version, can also be embarrassing. So often, an adult is still being called by a ridiculously inappropriate name, obviously a carry-over from childhood.

Baptism and Godparents

In some cultures, the custom of connecting the child to the religious heritage of the family is still honoured. In the Christian ceremony of christening or baptism, a child is given back to God from whence it came and the parents promise to bring it up in the tradition they consider theirs.

Also in Christian families, a man and a woman chosen by the parents undertake to supervise the child's moral and spiritual education. The godparents, as they are called, often have more influence on the child than the parents, to whom it will more than likely turn a deaf ear after a certain age, when 'familiarity breeds contempt'. Like so many other old customs, this too has fallen into disuse or lost its original significance. As a result, the moral and spiritual education of children all over the world has suffered.

Since children learn more from adults' example than from their words, both parents and godparents must pay careful attention to their own words, acts and attitudes if they expect children to develop into responsible adults.

It is also very important for parents to bear in mind a fact that is too often overlooked, that a baby is a developing person and should not be treated as a baby for ever. A simple way to avoid lapsing into the habit of continuing to 'baby' children is to determine not to use baby talk from the very beginning, even during pregnancy, either when referring to the child or talking to it. It is preferable to adopt an attitude suitable for conversing with an intelligent person, which could help the child to become one. That does not mean using complex sentences, long words, or intricate phrases. It means stating what needs to be said as directly and simply as possible. In other words, giving clear messages instead of confused ones, which can only lead to pain. This attitude will reassure the child that its parents are honouring and accepting him or her as a person.

A very common complaint of many adults is that they are treated by their parents as if they were still children. This situation can be most frustrating. In some cases, to their intense dismay and embarrassment, it even causes them to behave as children whenever they are with their parents, however hard they determine not to revert to infantile behaviour. Another effect is to make them feel that their worth as individuals is not recognized. Far too many people tell me that they never felt they were taken seriously, or that their parents never really heard them. They were treated as if they were extensions of their parents, like arms and legs, doing their bidding, instead of living separate individual lives.

Chapter 6

THE
BIRTH CHART

An astrological birth chart can sometimes help parents to find out a little more about their newly born child.

In many countries, primarily in Asia, a chart is drawn up as soon as a baby is born. It is treated as a map indicating areas that need to be understood by the parents or those responsible for bringing up the child to help it to attain its full potential.

A birth chart interpreted by a competent astrologer can point out possible character traits, inclinations, strengths and weaknesses of a newborn baby. For instance, the chart could reveal the possibility of a child being unusually sensitive, in which case the parents are alerted to the inadvisability of administering harsh discipline. It could show that a child is likely to have a certain ability or talent which the parents can then be prepared to encourage instead of propelling it into avenues of their own choosing. Or again, it could show that a child is apt to be deceitful and will need very firm but understanding correction of this undesirable trait.

Astrology can be useful so long as the astrologer is capable, and so long as parents treat the chart as a general guide to a child's potential rather than allowing it to give them fixed expectations. It must be remembered that a chart can be lived out in many ways.

One of the most important points to bear in mind, and one that will help to prevent parents from causing undue hardship to their children, is to remember that each child is an individual with different specific needs from either the other siblings or the parents. When birth charts for each member of a family are obtained, these differences show up very clearly. Parenthood can then be an adventure in discovering the essential selfhood of each child and helping them to fulfil their potential. This should be the aim of every parent instead of rearing children to be little carbon copies of themselves or to be the successful people that they themselves have failed to become.

If this understanding attitude is adhered to, true education can proceed, whereby the child's innate qualities are recognised, drawn out and encouraged, instead of the parents projecting onto their children their own expectations and demands and, in so doing, suppressing and stifling their separate individuality.

Astrological birth charts can help parents understand their children; they can also be very useful in indicating those areas of an adult's personality that need to be worked on. But it is not advisable to consult an astrologer or a chart for every small decision or plan. Astrology can become a crutch for some types of people, making them far too dependent and incapable of using their own reasoning in making decisions. Anyone or anything which becomes a crutch eventually assumes control over the one who has come to rely on it.

A birth chart interpreted by a reputable and knowledgeable astrologer can act as a map indicating the tendencies, strengths and weaknesses from past lives to be balanced and realigned in the present one. When used as an aid to character analysis, it can be a most helpful instrument. When it is used to foretell the future it can have a negative effect. Like any means of prediction, it can prevent a person from realising that he is at liberty to alter future events in his life by working hard to eliminate his weaknesses and change his attitudes. It is foolish to try to look into the future just as it is of no avail to hark back to the past with regrets or longings. To quote Baba again, 'The present is the product of the past, but it is also the seed of the future.'

Chapter 7

THE EARLY
YEARS: PRE-PUBERTY

On entering the world at birth, at some level, a child is probably aware of its forthcoming life-pattern, though as yet lacking the ability necessary to carry it out consciously.

It should be borne in mind that the parents are usually almost exclusively responsible for the early training of their children. So it is they who either start them out on a course designed to help them to achieve their potential or, as is unfortunately so often the case due to lack of knowledge and guidance, rear them in the haphazard manner in which they themselves were raised.

Parents faced for the first time with an unknown entity in the form of their newborn baby often lack the necessary knowledge to help with its development. I shall never forget how helpless I felt when I first held my newly born elder daughter. Here was this little unknown person about whom I knew nothing. I had not the faintest idea what to do with her. If only a list of instructions had come with her to explain what she needed from both her father and me to help her use this life to the best possible advantage.

At birth, a child relies almost totally on its parents to supply all its needs. It is obvious that parents must provide it with food, shelter and loving care until it grows independent. But beyond these practical necessities there exists a huge blank to be filled;

all this is frequently accomplished in a hit-and-miss fashion as the child inevitably grows towards maturity. To the majority of parents it is a bewildering prospect. Usually, they have only the memories of their own childhood and their parents' influence to guide them with their own children. In this way, many patterns of child-rearing are handed down from generation to generation, some positive and some negative in their effect upon the child's development.

It is the reaction of the growing child to the entire environment, including everyone and everything in it, that determines its progress or the reverse.

Parents are authority-figures while a child is helpless to fend for itself. But if this parental control continues beyond childhood into adulthood, it prevents the developing youth from taking responsibility for his own life. He will be rendered too dependent, first on the parents and then on others in positions of authority.

However, if a child is to grow into an independent, responsible and mature adult, he needs to be taught that there is a higher authority than his parents that he can contact within his own heart. He needs to understand that this inner authority, or High C, is his own true self. It is, therefore, more reliable than any other guide, especially his own ego or personality.

As the child grows old enough to understand, he can be led by the parents to seek guidance from this inner source. They can teach him to sit quietly and listen for thoughts or images to enter his mind in answer to his questions or appeals for help. When parents set the example by themselves following this practice, and are willing to sit with the child and initiate him or her into the habit, the results are often remarkable. Most children take to it very naturally if they are taught the process before they come under the influence of others, particularly their peers, who may ridicule such behaviour.

When this practice is successfully initiated and faithfully followed, by the time of puberty the child will be ready to cut the inner ties to the parents and continue more and more to seek the help and guidance of the High C, who alone knows best his destiny and needs.

Parental control and guidance of pre-pubescent children are largely missing, primarily because, in many families both parents need to work outside the home to support their desired life-style. The children of working parents are left to the care of baby-sitters, or older siblings, or in a nursery school, for far too many hours each day. They are often under the direct care of their parents for fewer hours than with non-family personnel. The result is that there is no conformity of supervision or training: children are exposed to one set of rules during the day and a different set when they are with their parents, causing them to receive confusing mixed messages.

To further complicate the scene, children whose parents are separated or divorced are invariably reduced to being mere pawns, caught in a cross-fire of continued arguments, or as the objects of competition by each parent for their love and affection.

Children brought up by single parents do not have the problems caused by conflicting types of discipline, so often the case when the mother and father have different priorities, or their views on child-rearing are at variance. But, when one or other parent is missing from their everyday life, they suffer by being deprived of the two distinct role models of masculinity and femininity to help them in shaping their own future roles as men or women.

Practical instruction is badly needed to help all adults who have undertaken the care of children. They need to be shown how to help the child to develop its own inner qualities, acquire habits that will allow it to live more fully and enable it to contribute to the world with confidence and a deep sense of security that emanates from knowing its own true identity.

But any two prospective parents have themselves been trained in very different ways by their two separate families. It is therefore often extremely difficult for either of them to relinquish their own ideas of child-rearing in favour of their partner's. When their two sets of rules or guidelines are so different that they clash, the only recourse is to seek an entirely new set that has been proved to work well and that they can both accept.

I remember when our two daughters were young children, I was given a book by Ilg and Gessell on child-rearing in which the authors described the so-called 'normal' accomplishments at each age. It was a great relief to have even this much help as a guide and measure.

Nowadays, there are innumerable books available on many aspects of child-rearing as well as classes for prospective parents to attend together. They are then both exposed to the same new method, which helps to prevent conflict.

Many systems emphasise the physical and mental education, but very often omit the extremely important moral and spiritual training. It is the latter that is so necessary to prepare children to take their place as honest, caring and responsible world citizens who will improve the quality of life by their example instead of adding to the confusion already rampant throughout our world today.

When children are taught from the very start of their [earthly] lives to retain the original contact they all have with the High C, they are more apt to develop from their inner pattern, just as flowers and trees produce blooms and fruits according to their own species. Too often the innate pattern is stifled or deformed when the child is forced to conform to the ideas or beliefs of its parents and elders, whether they are appropriate or not.

Children are quick to detect the slightest trace of disapproval and will often suppress whatever does not evoke a positive response from their parents or guardians. Their very life depends on gaining approval from their parents; they will try very hard to earn it unless the demands are so severe that they force them to negate their own inner truth. In such cases, they will either rebel in an effort to express their right to their own identity, or withdraw within in an endeavour to protect their right to be themselves. Obviously, neither of these reactions can lead to healthy growth, balance or eventual maturity.

However, when parents have themselves learned to seek guidance from the High C, they are more likely to encourage their children to do the same. Those children whose parents have given them a living example of relying on the High C usually follow their lead and mature into responsible adults who continue to be guided in this way wherever they go. As Baba often says, only in this way can the world be changed for the better. Since the world is composed of people, as the people change, so will the world. To this end, he has initiated an extensive programme in which children from the age of 5 attend special classes specifically designed to teach them moral values and encourage them to keep in touch with the indwelling God-force for help and guidance.

His Education in Human Values programme for older children contains all the basic guidelines for a more effective and complete education. It includes the teaching of moral values in addition to the usual academic subjects now being exclusively taught in schools.

This programme has been accepted in one form or another by several state governments in India in addition to their usual school curriculum. Authorities in other parts of the world, too, are gradually paying attention to Sai Baba's educational programmes.

By such means, the children of the world can gradually be taught true values which will develop positive habits. When they mature and take responsible positions in their countries, a major step will have been taken towards a better world under their stewardship. Instead of instinctively following the behaviour patterns of their parents, they will be capable of making their own choices, which at times may not necessarily be in accordance with those of the parents.

The two motivating forces of instinct and free will often conflict in a person's life, causing great confusion, guilt, indecision and a host of other problems. The instinctive action dictated by time-honoured and proven habits of the group may lead to one type of behaviour; but, if it runs counter to either a person's desire or his beliefs about what is right, he may be drawn to two opposite types of behaviour. If he has a strong will, he may be able to stand firm by his own convictions. But, an unconscious guilt that he has deserted the instinctual mores of his heritage may be lurking in the background causing indecision.

Those who are not endowed with a strong will take the path of least resistance and follow the dictates of their particular family or group. They then often have an unacknowledged fear that by thus conforming they have denied expression to an important part of themselves. This is an undeniable loss and it too can cause guilt.

Parents and teachers are, therefore, faced with the necessity of steering a course between these two paths in training the children under their care. They need to define, first for themselves and then for the children, the true eternal values underlying all cultures, world religions and philosophies.

Baba has presented many of these tenets in the Education in Human Values programme. The five values that form the basis, *Sathya* (Truth), *Dharma* (Right Action), *Shānti* (Peace), *Prema* (Love) and *Ahimsā* (Non-violence) cannot exist separately from one another, for each is connected to all the others. All five are to be practised simultaneously to bring about harmony, balance and true maturity or wholeness. Actually, love is the most important of the five and each of the others can be attained only when it is combined with love as its most creative component.

But how can parents teach their children about love when they themselves may not have been taught either how to love or how to experience being loved? It has been proved that the most important aspect of bringing up children is love. But unless the true significance of that much maligned word is understood, many parents may not have the slightest idea of how to proceed.

To add to the confusion, it is well known that too much love of the wrong kind can be just as disastrous to the child as too little. Again, it is necessary to find that fine line between the two extremes. Children who have never received love are incapable of loving others and, worse still, of loving themselves or receiving love from others. But those who have been spoiled by doting parents are in an equally serious condition. They are often only interested in themselves and the instant gratification of their desires. They demand from everyone they meet the same crippling adulation they have become accustomed to receiving from their parents. When they do succeed in attracting it to themselves, they then become even more spoiled, self-involved and demanding; but, if they fail to receive it, they tend to become disgruntled, complaining and helpless grown-up children, a burden to their families and friends and to society in general.

So, how can parents avoid these major pitfalls of loving their children either too little or too dotingly, each equally crippling to the child in their different ways? The only way to successful parenting is to understand and constantly remember that all are one at the High C level, though the individual personalities are very different from one another.

Parents need first to recognise the High C in themselves and ask It to direct them, since It is far wiser and more truly loving than they are. But at the same time, they must also honour the High C as the true Self residing within the children under their care. Only then can they be instrumental in helping their children to reveal this same true Self hidden within them, just as a particular type of tree or flower is hidden within a seed or bulb, waiting to be activated and brought to maturity as flower or fruit.

If parents fall into the common trap of thinking that the children they have borne belong to them, they will be tempted to treat them more like possessions than separate individuals with their own life-pattern. This will lead to the erroneous practice of trying to control their every move, thought, word and deed in an attempt to mould them to fit their own image and to become replicas of themselves. This unfortunate tendency in parents has been the cause of a tremendous amount of suffering for hosts of children, as well as for their parents when the end result is estrangement.

Chapter 8

TECHNIQUES FOR USE
WITH YOUNGER CHILDREN

Many of the techniques presented in *Cutting the Ties that Bind* can be used very successfully by even quite young children. They are usually still in touch with their inner world and have not yet developed too much overlay to cut them off from contact with the High C. They are, therefore, free to adopt the various symbols and rituals with minimal questioning or resistance from their developing ego. They are also much more open to accepting that they can use their imagination, with which they are all generously endowed at birth, to supply them with the tools that can help them in their everyday lives. Very often children put adults to shame by calmly suggesting ways to solve problems, if they are asked. If they can be included in some of the family discussions and invited to participate in asking the High C to show them solutions to simple problems, they will carry this habit with them into adulthood instead of feeling at a loss, or insecure or helpless at difficult moments.

Children are so often underestimated, kept too dependent on their parents, or have their attempts to participate as individuals discouraged. Given a chance, they invariably prove to be in closer contact with the High C than the adults who have had the original contact overshadowed by outer authority-figures and, eventually, by their own ego.

The Maypole

The Maypole can be used by families to connect everyone in the group to the High C, which is common to all the members. A pole is imagined or visualised in the middle of the room with many different coloured ribbons attached to the top and hanging down all around it. Each person imagines going up to the pole, taking a ribbon of whatever colour he or she prefers and returning to their seat with it held loosely in the hand. The ribbons link each person to the top of the pole representing the joint High C.

A little girl in a workshop I was conducting piped up in an excited voice, 'Oh, Mrs Krystal, I tugged on my ribbon and the High C tugged back. I could really feel it, honest!' This illustrates how naturally and trustingly children accept such practices. They have not yet become separated from close contact with the High C and, unlike adults, with their more developed minds, are not as likely to be as critical, analytical or doubting.

As soon as each member of the family is linked to the High C by the ribbons, they can ask to be shown a symbol or image representing It to them. Children are quick to elicit a response from the High C. Some 'see' a light, others the figure of Jesus, Baba, an angel, a sun, moon or star or one of many other symbols. A visual symbol gives them a more definite form with which to make contact.

They can then ask the High C to send down each ribbon the kind of love that is available only from this inner source. By using their breath, they can breathe in the love and breathe out any feelings or thoughts that might be preventing them from letting the love flow into them from this truly loving part of themselves. They can then be encouraged to sigh or even gasp out any problems, sadness, hurt feelings or fear, and breathe in the wonderful love that can replace these negative emotions with a feeling of well-being.

Each family member can then ask to be shown in a way they prefer, say, via a picture, a thought or a feeling, the guidance or solution to the problem under discussion. It is often quite astonishing to hear what the children receive in this way. Frequently, when the various contributions are shared, a clear message is revealed signalling the next step to be taken towards a solution by all or some of the family. Many problems can be solved quickly with this technique. In addition, it unites the members of the family in seeking answers beyond the conscious mind and will.

Children brought up with the knowledge that this help is always available whenever they need it grow to maturity with a deep feeling of security instead of a frightening sense of insecurity so many adults carry with them throughout their lives, causing them great distress and a feeling of failure.

One tiny child surprised her mother one day by saying, 'Let's listen to Baba's voice and see what he has to say about it,' when a question arose involving a difference of opinion between them. In this case Baba was the symbol for the High C. Another child announced that he knew what he wanted and what his father wanted, but which was right? He suggested they both ask the High C to show them.

Children possess a powerful imagination unless, or until, it is dimmed or suppressed. They delight in being shown how to use it to help themselves, instead of in day-dreaming or in frightening thoughts, whenever they become aware of problems affecting them, in contrast to not being given the true facts to allay their fears.

If a particular member of the family is apt to be a distraction, the disturbing effect on the others can be greatly lessened if they all visualise or imagine a golden circle surrounding him or her on the floor. This will keep the distracting element inside their own territory and thus make it less likely to disturb the others.

The Figure Eight

Children also thrive on the use of the Figure Eight. They meet a great deal of aggression from other children, both siblings and peers, as soon as they are old enough to participate in pre-school groups and, later, in school. As with all other species, the pecking order soon comes into full force, and it is then often a matter of the survival of the most aggressive.

Children can be shown at an early age how to use their imagination to put a golden circle around themselves for protection and another around an attacking child, with a neon blue light flowing around the two circles to form the Figure Eight.

There are several other ways in which the Figure Eight can be used to help both parents and children.

Mothers with new babies are often exhausted from lack of sleep due to the baby waking many times during the night. Sometimes it cries for good reasons, such as hunger, pain, heat or cold. But it can also fuss for attention. At such times, the mother can visualise the Figure Eight around herself and the baby to reduce unnecessary demands.

One of the participants at a recent seminar I conducted, told the group how she used it when her grandson was in a hospital sharing a room with several other babies, one of whom was continuously crying and disturbing the others. She remembered the Figure Eight and put the fretful baby in one golden circle with the others in the opposite circle and visualised the blue neon light moving around in the form of a figure eight for a few minutes. To her delight and surprise, the baby stopped crying after only a minute or two and, when she went to its crib to check, it was sleeping peacefully.

The Figure Eight can also be used very successfully with quarrelling siblings. In this situation, the parent or other adult can visualise the Figure Eight around the two children to lessen the clash of wills.

Sometimes, there is a negative relationship between a child and one of its parents. If such is the case, the Figure Eight can be visualised around the two of them by the other parent. The child can also be taught to practise it himself. In addition, he can be encouraged to make contact with the appropriate Cosmic Parent to take the place of the difficult one and supply whatever is missing in that relationship. This technique is also very helpful for children who are being reared by a single parent and lack the role model that would normally be supplied by the absent one. The same applies to children of divorced parents. It can provide an inner source of security for children of a divided family.

The Triangle

In addition to the Figure Eight, it is also very helpful to use the Triangle whenever a child is physically or emotionally upset, angry, rebellious or out of control in some way. The parent, teacher, or other adult in attendance, merely thinks or visualises being at one end of the base of a triangle, point A. The child is then imagined as being at the other end, point B, with a beam of golden light connecting them across the base. Two more beams of golden light are imagined flowing up along both of their spines to meet at the apex of a golden triangle connecting them both to the High C at that apex. A symbol of the High C may present itself, but this is not essential. Sometimes a diffusion of light will be observed.

The exercise consists in asking the High C to pour down the parent's side of the triangle Its love, together with whatever else It knows the child needs at that time. The parent, with hands held palms open in the lap to indicate receptivity, breathes in the energy that will flow into him or her from the High C as soon as he or she asks for it. After a few minutes, with palms together and fingers extended, the parent directs the flow of energy he or she is receiving from the High C across to the child.

I have seen this simple exercise work miracles but, as with all the other techniques, it works only when it is actually practised. So often we try to force a solution with our own will rather than surrendering a situation to the High C and asking for Its help.

This exercise is, of course, not limited to use solely with children. It can be used at any time, in any circumstances and with any person. It is actually the utmost that anyone can do for another, since it gives the other person the opportunity to be linked to the High C and to receive from It whatever is needed at the time. It is absolutely safe and complete. In the event that the person is not open or willing to receive guidance from the High C, his free will is respected and nothing will be forced upon him. If he is receptive, he will be given whatever he needs – and this could well prove to be a need that neither he nor anyone else is aware of.

However, if it is obvious that someone needs something specific, then, of course, it can be requested of the High C. Everyone needs love, but especially the kind of love available from the High C, so that can always be requested. The one breathing it in and directing it will also benefit as it will augment his own human love. For in so far as we are willing to allow the High C's love to flow through us and then direct it to others, our own capacity to love is increased.

The Tree and Cosmic Parents

Children respond very well to the Tree meditation and become adept at calling on one or both of the Cosmic Parents, who together form the High C, whenever they need help and their human parents are either not available or incapable of helping.

I have led a whole group of children through this technique. First, each child asks the High C to show him a tree. He then imagines going up to the tree, putting his arms around it and hugging it. He then turns around with his back to it, falls back against the trunk and feels its strength and security. He then imagines being like a tree as it pushed its roots down into the earth to bring up whatever he needs from the Great Earth Mother.

He breathes in this nourishment and breathes out anything that is bothering him or creating difficulties in accepting what he is being offered.

He is then directed to visualise himself reaching upwards to the sky and the sun again breathing in whatever the sun, the Great Solar Father, has to give him, and breathing out anything that could be stopping him from receiving hs true needs.

When children are directed to ask the two Cosmic Parents to appear at either side of the tree, the Mother on the left, the Father on the right, they often come up with amazing personifications of these Inner Parents. This exercise can bring great relief to children who feel inwardly isolated, or not fully accepted by one or both of their parents, or who have lost one or both parents through death or divorce and lack the role model of the absent one. It is also a good preparation for the eventual puberty rites when a child needs to cut the ties to the human parents while retaining contact with the cosmic ones. By that time, he should already have begun to rely on these inner ones and the transition therefore is much smoother, with far less stress during the teenage struggle for independence from parental control.

Using the Jack to Overcome Fear

Many children are very fearful, whether or not they are conscious of it. So, when fear is a problem, the child can use the Jack to help him remove both the fear and its power over him and replace them with light. Since most children have played the game of jacks, they enjoy using this symbol for a new purpose.

Essentially, it entails the child imagining a large jack of golden light up above his head. He is instructed to imagine reaching up to pull it down, as if it is on a pulley, until it stops in front of his solar plexus. He is then led back in memory to a recent time when he was afraid of something and asked where in his body he felt the fear. Next, he observes how the fear looked or felt as he recollects it. He is then told to imagine that the centre of the jack is like a black hole in space and has the ability to eat up or destroy anything sent into it. It is delightful to watch children blow out the fear and breathe in the light that flows from all the points of the jack to fill in the space where the fear had been. They throw themselves into these activities with such enthusiasm that they derive results much more quickly than is usual with adults. Many children have successfully freed themselves from all kinds of fear in this way.

Nightmares

When children have nightmares of a fierce animal chasing or attacking them, or some other frightening event, they respond very well to the following technique. They can be told that they themselves have created the creature through their imagination, thoughts and fears. So, if they were able to think up a scary creature, they can just as easily make it disappear by picturing it becoming smaller and smaller until it is so small that it fits into the palm of their hand. Now that it is so much smaller than they are, they must surely be much more powerful than it is. Once they can accept that, one can offer them the choice of deciding to make it smaller still until it completely disappears, or to keep it as a toy to remind them that they no longer need to be afraid of it.

This technique teaches children to control their thoughts. They discover that they can use this ability in many different situations instead of reacting negatively to them.

The Beach Ball

When I gave a seminar at a camp in the mountains, some of the people who attended it had brought their children along for a holiday. One of the park-keepers informed the families that there were bears in the area. He warned them to be careful and not to wander too far from the campsite, especially at night, or to leave any food outside the cabins that could tempt the bears. This warning frightened some of the younger children so much that they were afraid to go alone to the outside lavatory. One of the mothers recalled the symbol of the Beach Ball I had described during the seminar as a protection from external menace. So she told her children to imagine all around them a large rainbow-coloured beach ball made of very hard rubber. She explained that anything that came up against the hard rubber would bounce right off and they would be completely protected and safe and need not be afraid as long as they had remembered to visualise the ball around them.

To her immense surprise, it worked. However, when one of the younger children woke up in the night, the fear returned. His mother reminded him to be sure to imagine his beach ball around him. He immediately followed her suggestion and again felt secure enough to go to the lavatory and back again, happy at his own bravery.

The Cylinder

Some children are very sensitive from the start and therefore unusually vulnerable to outside influences, both positive and negative. For these highly sensitive little ones, it is helpful to use the Cylinder. It can be visualised around a child by a parent until he is old enough to imagine it in place himself. First, the parent imagines the golden circle around the child on the floor and, using the imagination, or just thinking of it, pulls it up all around the child to form a cylinder of light that is permeable, but protects him from too strong an influence or energy. When he is protected in this way, he will not be so overpowered by external forces. This technique often enables a child to make decisions for himself instead of being swayed by more dominating people or customs, and especially by peer-group pressure.

The Scales and Signposts for Decision-Making

Scales

An effective way to help children or adults make the right decision is with the help of the Scales. Children can be shown a model or illustration of one consisting of a central shaft with a cross-beam from which hang two small cups or dishes. A symbol of each of the choices can be placed in each cup. The child is then told to turn his attention away from the inner scene for a minute or two and then look back quickly to see which of the bowls is lower. The symbol in the lower bowl weighs more heavily than the other one, signifying the decision that should be adopted.

Signpost

If there are more than two choices, the Signpost can be used instead of the Scales. The pointers represent the various possibilities.

Again, the child is instructed to look away as soon as he has visualised the Signpost and then look back quickly to see which direction is still clear, all the others having disappeared.

Once they have been exposed to these techniques, children are quick to contribute their own ideas, many of which are delightfully innovative. Their drawing and modelling ability can also be used to help them to remove any negative traits or attitudes. They can either draw or make a clay model as a symbol of each negative attitude and put it in the opposite circle of the Figure Eight. After the two-week practice, it can be destroyed in whatever way is shown by the High C.

The Mandala and Pyramid for Developing the Four Functions

What actually is education? According to one dictionary, it means, 'To lead, draw or bring out'. Thus education should draw out the true potential within each individual.

Everyone possesses four aspects, or functions, that comprise the personality, in addition to a fifth aspect, which is the spiritual, or real Self, though they may not all be equally well developed. They are: sensation or the physical aspect; intellect or thinking; emotion or feeling; and intuition or psychic ability. The attributes of each are:

1. *Sensation.* Sensation, or the physical function, pertains to the body, as distinct from the mind, emotions and spirit. It is expressed through the five senses of sight, hearing, touch, smell and taste.

2. *Intellect.* The intellectual function relates to learning, analysing, reasoning and thinking, and the ability to know and understand cerebrally.

3. *Emotion.* Emotion enables a person to experience subjective feelings of joy, sorrow, reverence, hate, love and many more.

4. *Intuition.* Intuition, or the psychic function, pertains to extraordinary, extrasensory and other non-physical mental processes.

5. *Spiritual.* The spiritual aspect relates to man's inner being, the timeless, formless and universal dimension of divinity.

All five aspects are equally important for realising the full potential of human life. True education encourages the child to develop all of them to the full. They are ready to be expressed in his life, though they may have been only partially conscious before. Unfortunately, the early training of a child too often suppresses these functions rather than helping to reveal them. Of course, they remain within, but buried so deeply in the subconscious that they may seem to be entirely missing.

In the present day, *sensation*, or the physical function, is usually well developed and many people are slaves to the body with its five senses, its appetites or addictions, and the endless desires it generates. Correct education should teach the child to be in control of his body, not to be in thrall to it.

The *intellect* also is more developed in a greater percentage of the world population than was formerly the case. It is strongly emphasised in the majority of education systems, often at the expense of the *emotional* function, which has consequently suffered the most by being repressed or suppressed to an alarming degree. This loss of full expression of true feeling is the root cause of the proliferation of violence and the appalling lack of concern for the welfare of others in a vast number of people. In most of the present systems, children are taught very little about this aspect of themselves. Lacking adequate training, they live with absolutely no concern for others, and engage in vandalism and all the other acts of violence that have become prevalent throughout the world.

Awareness of *intuition*, or our psychic ability, has been undergoing a recent renaissance. Whereas in the past it was relegated to the fringe areas of society, and in some ways was suspect or too occult for most people to accept, it is now enjoying a resurgence of interest. Training in intuition is even being offered as a respectable and therefore acceptable subject in some colleges and universities in America. This might soon be the case in Europe, too, perhaps.

Sadly, the *spiritual* aspect involving the ability to express the innate spark of divinity is largely overlooked in favour of the more tangible and material functions of sensation and intellect, or even of the psychic ability with its more spectacular appeal.

Education, if it is to become a complete system designed to develop the potential of the whole person, needs to address all five human functions.

The Mandala

The Mandala is a symbol used to help individuals and families to balance the five innate functions. It is used to tone down the over-developed functions and to emphasise, or enhance, the under-developed ones. In fact, we use two different symbols for this: the Mandala is more visual and the Pyramid more experiential, but their functions are very similar.

Essentially, the Mandala[1] comprises a circle like a full moon reflecting the sun. The moon represents the individual and the sun the universal God-force. It is divided into eight pie-shaped wedges, with alternate ones forming a four-coloured Maltese cross, the other four remaining blank. Yellow is at the top and directly opposite at the bottom is green. At right angles to this pair are rose to the left and blue to the right. The colours represent the different functions: yellow symbolises intuition or psychic ability, green stands for sensation or the physical aspect, rose indicates emotion or feeling, and blue represents intellect or thinking.

In the centre there is a diamond symbolising the perfection of the spiritual function emanating from the inner core of divinity. Like a diamond, or a crystal, reflecting the light of the sun, refracting it into all the colours of the rainbow, it mirrors the true Self within everyone. It is complete and perfect and, when requested, will flow into each of the other functions to energise them and bring them all into perfect balance in the person's life.

A rheostat, or dimmer, is imagined behind each colour. Those functions that are overdeveloped need to be dimmed and those that are weak need to be increased. The exercise ends with all the colours equally luminous so that the desired message to balance them is impressed on the subconscious, which can then make it possible.

Pyramid

An alternative method for balancing the four functions is for the person to imagine he is standing inside a pyramid. Each wall is painted one of the four colours: yellow, green, rose or blue. He starts by facing the wall depicting the colour of his weakest function for several minutes, followed by each of the other walls for less time in relation to their weakness or strength. In this way, a very cerebral person, who is invariably weak in his emotional or feeling aspect, would first face the rose-coloured wall; while a very sensation-orientated person, weak in intuition, would begin by facing the yellow wall, and so on.

[1] For a detailed description see *Cutting the Ties that Bind*, Chapter 14.

The crystal or diamond is visualised at the top of the pyramid reflecting the rays of the sun and refracting them like a rainbow cascading down.

Children enjoy practising these two exercises, particularly when they are shown that each family member may not have the same strong and weak functions, which is the reason they are different from one another, though not necessarily superior or inferior. Each has a contribution to make and they all need to strengthen their own weak areas rather than rely on the stronger ones among the family.

These differences make it clear why various people within a family communicate better with some of the members and not as well with others. Those who have the same functions well developed speak the same language and therefore get along easily together. However, with those in whom the opposite functions prevail, there is always a danger that each will rely on the stronger functions of others instead of making an effort to strengthen their own weaker ones. Such symbiosis can lead to stultification rather than growth. Each member needs to be encouraged to develop his own four functions to the fullest extent. This can be accomplished with the help of the High C or Diamond Self.

Children should never be unfavourably compared to others, whether friends, siblings or relatives. To do so results in unnecessary competition and causes dislike, envy and jealousy between them. It is preferable to concentrate on discovering where each child needs to improve, and then to encourage them to help each other to do so.

A comforting thought is that the High C can more easily direct a person through the weaker functions buried in the subconscious as they are less subject to control by the ego. Those talents or activities of which a person is proud are more likely to be under the control of the ego. If a person can do something well, they tend to become conceited, whereas, in failure they are much more likely to ask the High C for help.

Children must be encouraged to ask questions instead of having their natural curiosity suppressed by parents who are often too busy to take the time or make the effort to help them to find answers. The questioning attitude helps to develop discrimination, and children are then less prone to influence by mass hypnosis or mass hysteria in any form. A questioning attitude is an inner tool that can help one to make conscious decisions instead of succumbing to outer conditioning or coercion. Too many young people have difficulty in making decisions, a situation that leaves them vulnerable to all forms of manipulation. They should be taught to use their own faculties to determine a course of action. Even if that path ultimately leads to a mistake, it will not have been a loss for they will never forget the mistake that taught the right course of action. This method of learning from personal experience, including failure, instead of from other people's advice, is always more lasting. Because a lesson has been learned in action, it becomes a part of the person. Seeking the advice of others who may not be reliable or always available often leaves a person at a complete loss.

The daily habit of asking for direction from the High C should be encouraged so that it becomes natural to turn to It for help at any time. When this habit is established from early childhood, and strengthened by the living example of parents, there will be far less overlay of negative conditioning to remove later in life.

Chapter 9

PUBERTY RITES

It is customary in some isolated societies, as it was in most ancient cultures, to remove adolescent boys and girls from the parental home and place them under the care of the older and wiser men and women of the group. These elders provide more intensive instruction in preparing the young people for their approaching roles as adults. They are then tested, often quite severely according to our present standards, to determine if they have developed the necessary understanding and skills to take their places as responsible members in the group. This custom makes a deep and lasting impression on the young people. It also breaks the constricting bond to their parents and allows them their first experience of independence.

The actual puberty rites vary considerably from culture to culture. A modern version of this type of ritual has been received from the High C, and it too can very effectively sever the close bonds to each parent. It sets the boy or girl free to take responsibility for their life by consulting their inner guide, the High C.

This severance from parents, or authority-figures, whether or not they are still alive, can be undertaken at any age after puberty, but naturally, it is easier to discard old patterns earlier rather than later in life. So, when the cutting is accomplished at the recommended time, at or near the age of puberty, there are fewer layers of conditioning to remove.

If the training of the children has proceeded along the lines described thus far, when they become young adults, they will be better equipped to live free from external coercion through the guidance they receive from within.

By the time youngsters reach marriageable age, they should be sufficiently mature and independent to choose a suitable mate with whom to start a new family. If each partner is Self-reliant, there is less danger of either one leaning on the other. Each will have learned to lean on the High C, common to them both. Such unions result in relatively intelligent parents who, in their turn, will apply to their own children what they themselves have been taught, thus breaking the old chain of negative conditioning handed down from their forebears. Parents who use this method to become consciously aware of their actions, and who unite in consulting the High C, will have far fewer problems, both in their marriage as well as with their responsibilities as parents.

Chapter 10

LOVE

Love is such a little word to express or contain so vast and complex an emotion.

Love is the primary need of every child, and it continues to be avidly sought throughout life by everyone, consciously and unconsciously. And yet, it is so often misunderstood.

Baba says that his love, and therefore the love of the indwelling God in everyone, is very different from the love expressed by most people. His love is expansive, unselfish, non-judgemental and completely accepting of each person as he or she actually is, with all their faults. Most people's love, on the other hand, is more often than not constricting, selfish, smothering, or controlling. Many people have not been given the kind of parental love they needed in order to thrive, for the simple reason that their parents did not receive it from *their* parents, and therefore did not understand how to express it.

For a surprising number of people, love is synonymous with sexual attachment. Many of the couples with whom I work cite this confusion as the main problem in their relationship. It is also one of the causes of incest, which is at present surfacing as a serious problem as this previously subterranean subject is being aired, and more people are becoming increasingly willing to deal with its presence in society. If the only way a person knows how to express their feelings is through sex, then that will be the only avenue through which they can offer their love to their children. However, an incestuous parent is likely to be filled with guilt which he might vent in anger on the very child who elicited his reaction. So many young children are bewildered by a parent suddenly turning against them because of the inability to love them in any way other than sexually.

It is particularly necessary for adolescents to be taught that there is, indeed, a difference between love and the sexual sensations they are beginning to be aware of as they grow. They need to know that these two sorts of feelings are not necessarily always experienced simultaneously, as is so often believed.

The love that emanates from the High C is a potent energy that can be expressed through any or all functions. It is polarised and therefore creative according to the function through which it is expressed. So, when it is expressed as sex, and creates children, it involves the sensation function related to the body and connected to the five senses, and can be stimulated by any or all of them.

Through the feeling function, love is expressed as affection, tenderness, empathy and compassion, which all emanate from the heart and create friendship and caring for others.

When people are only able to think their love, it is expressed through the head and intellect and is not warm, reassuring or compassionate, but cold and often calculating. It is creative on the mental level, spawning ideas, plans, designs and concepts that then have to be made manifest on the material level.

By way of the intuition or psychic outlet, love allows a person to tune into another dimension, and understand how other people are feeling, their moods, their problems and the events in their lives. It manifests itself creatively in wondrous inventions.

It can easily be seen that the love-force is many-faceted and can take a variety of different forms. The more facets of the human personality through which it is expressed, the more fulfilled the person.

But how does one express love in these varied ways without instruction? That is a very serious problem and one that is rapidly becoming crucial.

As love is energy, it must be free to flow. If it is blocked or repressed, it can change into its opposite, hate. One of the commonest ways to stop its flow is by using it for selfish purposes. Yes, we all need to love ourselves but if it stops there so does the flow. Love must be given if we are to continue to receive it.

For various reasons, very few people know how to love. If they were not taught how to love, or given positive loving role models to follow in childhood, they need methods to teach them. Several techniques designed specifically for that purpose have been given in this work.

One technique involves the use of the Mandala or Pyramid described in Chapter 8. It requires concentration on the rose-coloured wedge of the mandala, or the rose wall of the pyramid, both representing emotion. Consciously breathing in the rose colour stimulates the feeling function through which love can be expressed.

The Tree technique is useful in connecting a person to the loving Cosmic Parents, the two aspects of the High C. It involves breathing in the love each Cosmic Parent offers when asked, and breathing out any blocks that may be preventing its acceptance. This love can fill the void left from the lack of love often experienced since childhood.

But, by far the most effective way to give and receive love, judging from my own experience and from observing the people with whom I work, has been one I inadvertently learned when we were hi-jacked[1]. Since the actual nature, or essence, of the High C is love, what better instructor, not only to teach it, but also to give it copiously when asked to do so? When the High C is asked to give the gift of love and, when it flows into you to be directed to others, the flow is unending. Not only does the recipient benefit from it, but so does everyone with whom it is shared.

A very helpful habit for people to adopt is to take a few minutes at the start of the day to ask the High C to think, speak, feel, act and especially to love through them all day. It can then send Its essence, love, through all the available avenues of body, mind, emotions, psyche and spirit.

---

[1] In *Sai Baba: The Ultimate Experience*.

Chapter 11

PARENTAL CONTROL

Many parents try to control their children by expecting them to live out their own unfulfilled dreams and aspirations, hoping in that way to gain vicarious satisfaction.

This attitude is not at all helpful, either to parents or to children. Parents need to express as fully as possible their own talents and ambitions. No one, not even their own children, can do that for them, and children can be seriously harmed by being forced into the parental mould. Many people's lives have been distorted due to the exacting expectations of their parents. They become frustrated and bitter when they are unable to live their own lives, according to their own inborn ability.

A similarly frustrating situation arises in families where parents expect their children, particularly their sons, to follow in the father's footsteps and become doctors, or lawyers, or take up the family business, whether they have the necessary attributes or not. Many lives are damaged by such parental control. Even worse is the resulting negative relationship between parents and children, whether the children follow the parents' wishes while harbouring resentment, or rebel and go their own way. If the latter is the case, the parents are often so upset that they disinherit them, refuse to see them, or make their lives miserable at every opportunity.

If only parents could try to discover the natural talents and inclinations latent in their children, they could then encourage them to express their undeveloped gifts to their fullest extent. Such an understanding attitude could prevent the too-frequent estrangement between parents and children from going too far.

It is helpful to remember that children are not possessions and do not belong to their parents. Since most couples have elected to bring children into the world, their duty is to guide and teach them to the best of their ability. But they must avoid imposing their will on them, either to follow in their footsteps or to live out their own frustrated dreams. Rather, they should try to discover where their children's paths lead them and help them to travel in their different ways.

Quite often one of the reasons for such domination originates in a family heritage where the rules and behaviour models are passed down the generations without the necessary adaptation to fit them to changing times. Customs and heritage are useful only if they meet the needs of their adherents. Otherwise, they can be likened to a prison in which children are confined, with their parents acting as the gaolers.

Equally serious problems can be caused by parents if they try to exert their will in the choice of their children's marriage partners. Too often a marriage is doomed to fail either because it was forced on the two people concerned by family pressure, or because it was not approved by one or both sets of parents.

In India and other countries where arranged marriages have been customary for centuries, there is an attempt to match the two prospective mates in temperament, background, life-style, horoscopes and religious beliefs. Many of these alliances are successful, though many are not, especially in the big cities, where Westernisation has eroded traditional values and introduced new expectations of marriage. There are even reports of dowry deaths, where young brides are killed to free the groom to remarry and benefit from a second dowry.

The job of all parents should be to help each child in their care to remove the dark cloaks of negativity gathered through many lifetimes. They obscure the true Self, which is a fragment of the Divine. But before this is possible, both parents need to clear away their own old overlay. By initiating both these tasks simultaneously, parents and children can be free to grow together towards reunion with their real Selves.

But too many people lack even an elementary concept of their own divinity, let alone the possibility of recognising It, seeking

Its guidance or eventually becoming one with It. As Baba tells us, as long as we seek outside ourselves for guidance, truth and fulfilment, we will be doomed to disappointment. We will be drawn this way and that, lured by the myriad temptations of the world in which we live, to assuage our appetites and achieve our desires. But desires are spawned by the body, mind and emotion sheaths in which our real Self resides. They can provide only temporary relief.

Again, 'Seek ye first the Kingdom of heaven and all other things shall be added unto you' is the answer. We limit what we are able to receive by being too attached to what we think we want. By relinquishing our desires we eventually become open to receive much more than we dreamed possible. If, in addition, we can train ourselves to hold what we are given lightly and without attachment or a sense of possession, our lives will be enhanced and we will cease to be imprisoned or shackled by our own anxious grip on them.

This concept does not imply that we should be careless or irresponsible regarding our material possessions. It is helpful to consider all that we own as being only lent to us for a certain unknown period of time, and to be ready to return it in at least as good a condition as it was when we received it, preferably, improved by our care. Parents should also extend this attitude of mind to their children, who are by no means possessions. Parents do not own them but merely elect to care for them until they are able to seek guidance from the Source within them. At that time, they should be relinquished to their inner mentor. The urge to continue carrying their responsibility, assumed at birth, should be resisted.

As long as we seek satisfaction or fulfilment in the outer world, composed as it is of temporary personalities, experiences and objects, we and our children will either be doomed to disappointment when we do not receive what we so avidly seek, or we will spend our entire lives in envy and hatred of others who are the recipients of the things we crave. If, on the other hand, our fondest desires are satisfied, we may spend our lives in fear and anxiety at the prospect of losing them.

Chapter 12

HOW
TEACHERS CAN HELP

So far, only the parental role in educating children has been considered, since parents represent the first influence in a child's life. Teachers also have an important and responsible role to play in encouraging children to develop morally as well as teaching them academic subjects. Teachers should extend the parents' initial teaching and simultaneously share that task with them. These two sets of authority-figures are usually those that have the strongest and most lasting effect on children. This is illustrated by the many stories of successful people who have given credit to a parent or one particular teacher who ignited their latent inner flame.

Many teachers with whom I have worked have told me how they were able, subtly, to introduce into their class work some of the techniques from *Cutting the Ties that Bind* without taking away time from the regular curriculum, and with excellent results.

The Maypole

For instance, the Maypole can be visualised by the teacher to give all the students the opportunity to be linked to the High C if and when they are ready to make this connection. When this symbol is used regularly, the tone of the class is raised, as it has the ability to lift the consciousness to the highest common denominator of the group. In that way, it allows the superior energy, wisdom and love from the collective High C to be activated. If, in addition, the teacher accepts the High C as the real teacher within them all and himself, instead of personally assuming that role, the entire class will benefit from the superior guidance both he and they will receive.

The Circle of Golden Light

The Golden Circle visualised around any conflicting individual who may be present in a family group can also be used very successfully by a teacher to calm a hyperactive child who may be disrupting a class. The circle, with a radius roughly the length of the child's arm with fingers extended, is visualised on the floor around the disruptive child. This simple device will contain him and his negative energy, and it can also act as a calming influence on him. To begin with, it should be repeated several times a day. The energy thus regularly invested in this symbol will become so strong that the child will be influenced to behave quite differently.

Some of the most difficult children for a teacher to handle in a classroom are those who are hyperactive and those who have been emotionally traumatised or abused and who vent their frustrations on others to relieve their own tension. The Golden Circle will contain their disruptive energy and give them the much-needed sense of security they lack.

I had suggested this technique to one young teacher who, quite some time later, told me that she had just recently taken a course on special education methods at her local university. In one of the sessions, the instructor informed the class of the recent discovery that hyperactive children need to be contained, or provided with boundaries, since these had not been clearly delineated for them by their parents. He reported that when their feet were placed in a cardboard box during class, their conduct improved considerably. She laughed and volunteered the information that the Golden Circle I had given her worked even better, and was also less of a stigma for such children, who were already the subject of too much negative attention.

Initially, they are helped without consciously knowing that anything is being done for them. After the technique has started to take effect and the results become observable, the child can be told about the Golden Circle and given the opportunity to imagine it around himself.

The human values from Baba's EHV programme outlined earlier, can be woven into the learning material and illustrated by the children in essays and reports. Truth can be taught as the basis of all subjects, as can right action, peace, love and non-violence. The addition of these principles will enrich the curriculum and give the children a much-needed foundation of practical standards by which to work and play.

In this programme, one of the exercises is called Silent Sitting. It is a term replacing the more controversial 'meditation'. This exercise can be practised daily as soon as the children have assembled. It need continue for only a few minutes to allow everyone in the class to settle down after their journey to school. It can then be suggested to the class that at any time during the day it is helpful to withdraw within to make conscious contact with the inner guidance available to everyone when they seek it. For instance, if they are having difficulty with a particular subject, they can be assured that if they sit quietly and ask to be shown how to proceed with it, they will receive directions either in the form of a thought, a picture or a sudden memory. With practice, children become adept at seeking help in this way and often come up with surprising answers to their questions.

One little boy, with whom I was working, spontaneously announced one day that he had always known he had a doctor inside himself on whom he could call for help whenever he was sick. Besides that, he continued, he also knew he had another hidden part of him from whom he could ask for help whenever he was having difficulties with spelling, which he confessed was not exactly his favourite subject.

Children only need to be given hints that they have within them untapped resources. They are quick to apply this knowledge and, in the process, gain in self-confidence as they discover how well it really works.

I always refer to the techniques I have been given as a tool-kit for use in daily living. Children need tools that really work to help them to cope with the many varied experiences they will be facing in their lives. When they discover how well they work, they are usually enthusiastic about them.

Another of Baba's programmes is *sevā*, or service, to the community. This, too, can be undertaken by both groups and individual children. In many schools, a class will adopt another class in a very poor area. The children are encouraged to collect toys and clothing that they have outgrown. These are then delivered to the needy children at the adopted school.

Other schools, and some families, arrange to take responsibility for a school or a child in a less developed part of the world or in a disaster area.

Our two daughters each had a series of 'sisters' in need of help in other countries. They used to write to them and send them needed articles, such as clothing, books and toys. Sharing in this way trains children to consider the needs of less fortunate people. Helping and caring for others encourages them to be less self-centred.

With very little encouragement on the part of parents or teachers, children can produce many excellent and practical ideas for helping others. They learn to appreciate what they have rather than taking things for granted as people so often do nowadays.

None of the above suggestions need steal much time from the general academic curriculum. When such programmes are launched, the improved attitudes and behaviour of the class will more than compensate for the time and energy expended.

The Ceiling on Desires programme already described can also be introduced into some of the classes. A great deal of waste takes place in our schools, not only of materials, but of time and energy. If children can be shown that they will all have more time and energy to devote to the activities they enjoy if they trim down such waste, it can give them an incentive to do so. Unnecessary talking, day-dreaming, inattentiveness, asking irrelevant questions, quarrelling and other wasteful habits steal time and energy from other activities.

When these ideas are explained to children in a clear and simple way, with examples to which they can relate, they often surprise parents and teachers with their co-operation and imaginative ideas. Parents and teachers can nurture children's innate creativity by giving them a few suggestions to get them started. It is also extremely important to praise their efforts for, with a little encouragement, children are quick to meet new challenges.

Chapter 13

ADDICTIONS

Parents and teachers are increasingly faced with serious problems connected to the various addictions, even among children of primary school age. Widespread abuse of these addictive substances appears to be symptomatic of the current decline in values. It is also a symptom of the underlying lack of love in the lives of so many adults and children preventing them from feeling recognised as worthwhile individuals.

Instinctively, people seek a means of escape from pain, whether it is physical, mental, emotional or spiritual. However, any type of pain is really a safeguard, or warning, alerting them to the presence of an unresolved problem and giving them an opportunity to address it.

We are currently being bombarded by the media with news of natural disasters: earthquakes, floods, drought, famine and cyclones, as well as wars, riots, epidemics, murders, rape, child abuse and a host of other horrors, not to mention pollution, the greenhouse effect and the holes in the protective ozone layer.

The effect of this daily barrage is an emotional overload. Individuals are not equipped to deal with so many enormous multiple problems for which they can see no obvious solution, especially on a personal level. It is as if they are overdosing on horrors, causing many to suppress their feelings and become numb as a means of self-protection. The result of this reaction is the hardening of the heart and the suppression of sympathy and compassion. This situation is evident today when usually loving and concerned individuals scarcely turn a hair at hearing or seeing instances of violence because they feel totally incapable of handling them emotionally.

Problems can be a challenge when their solution is a possibility. But without that hope the accumulation becomes too heavy. With no visible means of dealing with it, every avenue of escape from the oppressive burden is desperately sought. These hoped-for panaceas include the many addictions which hold out the promise of relief. Addictive substances react on different people in different ways. Some sedate the users, with the result that problems are not felt as keenly. Others overstimulate, and keep people so frenziedly active that they have no time to dwell on anything for very long, let alone any problem.

But these substances are merely palliatives. They do not heal a condition or solve a problem, so the situation they were supposed to alleviate remains and is there when, in time, their distracting or numbing effects wear off.

There is another serious side-effect of resorting to these means of escaping pain. In addition to their being addictive, and eventually enslaving their users, there appears to be no certain cure. Once addicted, it is not only extremely difficult to break the habit, but even when, with professional help, they are freed from one addiction, they frequently fall prey to another.

It seems clear from the many cases of continued dependence on such 'crutches' that there are addictive personalities. This personality trait can be traced to many different causes, such as the early patterning by parental and family behaviour. If children become used to seeing their parents, or other authority-figures, turn to alcohol, cigarettes, pills, drugs or other compulsive habits for relief of stress, they will gradually develop the habit of relying on the same or similar means of escape themselves.

Other cases of addictive behaviour can be traced to a hereditary imbalance in the body, such as a lack or excess of certain chemicals and minerals. Many alcoholics have a family history of sugar imbalance.

But, above and beyond these more obvious causes, I have recently been shown others of a more serious nature. Everything in the universe has an identifying tone, scent, essence or wavelength.

We often refer to people or things being in tune or 'in sync' with one another, or having a rapport. We are all creating thought-forms all the time for the simple reason that we rarely stop thinking except during deep sleep, or unconsciousness. When we habitually think about something, or give our attention to it, we gradually strengthen it with our energy, for it takes energy to think, speak, act and live.

When many people repeatedly direct their attention to something, even more energy is invested in it, with the result that it gains power over individual people by eventually becoming stronger than them.

These huge collections of energy contained in thought-forms can be likened to archetypes. They possess so much power that they are stronger than the individuals who have used their thoughts and energy first to create them and then to maintain them. Some are positive in their effect, others are negative, depending upon the quality of the original thought. Some of these negative pockets of energy are so powerful that they are almost tangible. They can be felt as a black cloud in the atmosphere, or attached to a particular location, or emanating from a building.

Some people carry these archetypes and are controlled by them, often quite unconsciously. Since they are larger than life, the individuals under their influence are helpless, having given away their power to these impersonal creations.

When people attempt to escape from pain through addictions, they often unconsciously tune into the multiple archetypes linked to the addictions and, once connected, find themselves utterly helpless to free themselves from these forces. This type of control is one of the causes of failure to overcome dependence on these means of escape from life's problems.

Children need to be taught that problems provide them with the opportunity to find solutions. Then they can look upon difficulties not as signals to escape, but as challenges enabling them to become stronger and free to live more fully.

Many children first experiment with addictive substances when they are learning to experience many new activities, or because of peer pressure, or from the desire to be popular or in fashion.

Parents and teachers need to inform children of the larger overlying forces connected to these habits. At the same time, they should be shown how to work out any problems they may have with the help of the High C. It is also helpful to explain that we are all too weak to overcome such powerful conditioning with our own familiar ego strengths. It takes the added energy of the High C to conquer the powerful archetypal control.

PART 2

One should free oneself from identification
with classes or races and conditions like
childhood, youth, adulthood and old age, of
genders like male and female.

Sri Sathya Sai Baba

Chapter 14

WHO ARE WE
AND WHY ARE WE HERE?

Baba says we are three people: the one we think we are, the body; the one others think we are, the mind; and the one we really are, divine and part of the universal God-force. He urges us to bring the first two into union with the real Self and make them all one, for in that way we can realise our true identity as Divinity.

Cutting the Ties that Bind dealt with the overlay of early conditioning by parents or guardians, teachers, ministers, friends, lovers and other authority-figures. From all these, most people have borrowed, either consciously or unconsciously, their beliefs, attitudes and reactions to events, people and experiences. This more obvious overlay needs to be dealt with first to detach ourselves from negative personal family conditioning.

After that has been accomplished, the subtler programming also needs to be released to reveal the real person beneath the many layers.

So this part of the book will show how to detach ourselves from larger, multiple and more complex systems which have conditioned us and our behaviour in specific ways.

Any type of patterning received from without may be in conflict with the true expression of ourselves. It obscures the spark of reality we all carry within us, our guide and teacher, our true self, so it prevents close communication with the High C. It is like getting a crossed line on the telephone, when it is difficult to hear and be heard because others are using the same line. The result is that only parts of the conversation are heard by either party. It produces confused communication caused by the many voices talking at once. When the inner remembered voices of parents or other authority-figures are constantly talking at a subliminal level, reception of messages from the High C is unclear.

Where did we come from and where are we headed? The answers appear to be that we originally emerged from the Godhead and are on our way back to merge into It. During this process, we are given the opportunity to become more fully conscious along the circuitous ways we travel, often straying far off the path, distracted by countless desires and attachments to the material world.

Why Are We Here?

Why are we here and what is this life meant to teach us? The answers to these questions are many and varied depending on who is asking and who is asked. I can write only of what I have been taught, through my work and, more recently, by Sathya Sai Baba, who elaborates on the teachings from all the ancient writings of sages and seers who were receptive to inspiration from beyond their own finite minds.

The consensus of opinion of these original sources is that we are here for two main reasons. First, we need to balance the energy we have at some time in the past clothed in thoughts, words and actions and launched into the world. Because our energy was sent forth in this way by our egos and wills, our thoughts, words and deeds will, like homing pigeons, return to roost in us. In that way we become the recipients of whatever we have initiated, giving us a chance to reap the rewards of all positive output, and to learn by suffering the experience of pain we caused others.

So another reason we are here is to learn to live in harmony with others, for we are all one at our common source. Whatever we do to others, we automatically do to ourselves at some stage in our long journey back to our original source.

To help us to understand what we are here to learn, Baba has enumerated various qualities we are here to develop. Those he mentions the most frequently are patience, tolerance, steadfastness and forbearance.

Patience

Patience and time are closely linked. There is a right time for everything, just as there are times for the sun and moon to rise and set and the four seasons to follow one another in sequence. A natural rhythm controls the events of the world and prevents chaos. According to Ecclesiastes 3:1, 'To every thing there is a season, and a time to every purpose under the heaven. A time to be born and a time to die; a time to plant and a time to pluck up that which is planted.'

When timing is forced, confusion results. If we can relax, surrender our will and ask to be shown when it is the right time for something to be set in motion, the steps to its fulfilment unfold at the right time and pace. It requires patience to be able to wait until that time arrives and to resist the temptation to try to hasten or defer its arrival by force. It must not be our time; we must await the High C's time.

Patience is also closely connected to desire. It is only when we want or do not want something that we lose patience, and can be disappointed about things that do not work out the way we want.

We should learn to trust the High C so completely that we can relax and wait patiently for It to bring about whatever is best for us, at the best time.

Tolerance

To be tolerant is to avoid being judgemental or critical, or condemning another person. It also means treating other people's beliefs with respect instead of ridiculing or despising them. 'Live and let live' sums up tolerance very simply and aptly. Tolerance also involves not reacting negatively to people, events or situations but remaining unruffled no matter what occurs. At the same time, we must have sufficient discriminatory powers so that we do not end up 'tolerating' wrong-doing or hurtful behaviour for the sake of being tolerant.

Steadfastness

Steadfastness means being so closely in touch with the High C and so completely guided by It that, in the face of any situation, resistance or coercion by others, we remain steadfast to our deepest truth.

Forbearance

I will quote Baba's description of forbearance:

Forbearance means refusal to be affected or pained when afflicted with sorrow and loss and the ingratitude and wickedness of others. These are all the results of one's own actions now recoiling on oneself, so look upon those who cause the misery as friends and well-wishers. The karmic burden has to be endured and eliminated. It is the law of cause and consequence.

Who is Your Puppeteer?

Who is your puppeteer, your own ego, someone else's ego, their will, or the High C? I shall always remember being given an opportunity to ask Baba to clarify this question when we were with him one year. Several members of the American organisation were present and the problem under discussion was how to deal with individuals who had very strong wills and who insisted on having their own way. Having myself experienced such a situation, I was anxious to know how to be sure whose will should be heeded, my own, someone else's or Baba's, which for me is tantamount to that of the High C. Sensing my question, Baba turned to me with a smile to encourage me to voice it, which I did. His answer was that, when in doubt, we should go to a quiet place and concentrate on asking within to be shown. He assured me that we would receive an answer within twenty minutes. Of course, many people expect a loud voice to proclaim the answer, or to receive it in some other equally dramatic way, but that is rarely the case. It can present itself through another person, in a book or an article, even in a song over the radio and, of course, via thought or memory. I find I do receive an answer whenever I ask sincerely from the heart.

A lifelong habit of being a puppet and playing various roles invented by others has its inception in childhood. Many children are expected to be like puppets, with their parents pulling their strings to make them dance to the tunes they play rather than their own.

The High C is the only entity who can know our real needs and therefore how best to direct us towards fulfilment and wholeness. To give power to another person, thing, custom, idea or regime is to court disaster by negating our real identity in trying to assume someone else's concept of it.

So we need to look very carefully at our behaviour to determine where we are still behaving like puppets and letting old concepts and childhood conditioning manipulate us. This arrangement can often continue through life, resulting in many of the different roles or 'hats' people assume, for one reason or another.

It is best not to be so attached to a role that it dominates or controls us. It is far better to assume an appropriate role for each different situation, and to remain free to exchange it for a more suitable one as need arises.

Not only do parents and other authority-figures play the puppeteer, but their 'puppets' also may be guilty of doing so and not only with their children, but also with anyone else who allows it.

The only trustworthy puppeteer is the High C. No one has the right to act as the Pied Piper expecting others to dance to the tune he chooses to play. But there is also the need to be alert to the reverse possibility, of becoming someone else's puppet.

The type of people most likely to become puppets are those who lack a clear self-image. Since they are not sure who they are, they easily fall into the trap of letting someone who is stronger and more secure propel them into an image or role, whether or not it fits them. This situation can continue for some time until a particular event jolts them into an awareness of what they are doing, at which time they may start to rebel. However, if the rebellion does not bring about freedom from constraint, they may go on being the puppet while suppressing the resulting anger, frustration and resentment. This creates an even more serious problem, as the negative emotions are directed to themselves and they begin to hate their own impotence.

Puppet theatres have been in existence for centuries. In many cultures they are a teaching device. Their forms may be different but the underlying theme is usually similar. The master puppeteer is always behind the scenes pulling the strings connected to the little puppets, controlling their movements to make them act out his wishes, as each scene depicts a common human situation. He can be likened to the High C and the puppets to the various aspects of the personality.

As infants, we start out with a particular family heritage designed to implement the learning we need to acquire to balance our actions during one or more past lives. The High C, or inner spark of divinity, is our real Self. The body, mind, emotions, ego and personality merely make up the sheaths that contain it. These sheaths are formed from our many earlier experiences. We were drawn back again and again into embodiment in this world to learn whatever we still had to understand. Every action results in a reaction, so we are all experiencing the reactions from all our past actions, both positive and negative, as well as initiating acts which will bear fruit in future lives. As soon as we are able to surrender our egos and wills to the High C and allow It to act through us, we will no longer incur any new karma. It will then be a case of the will of the High C working through us in our lives.

We all have free will and the High C always respects it and never interferes or uses coercion. We must reach a point where we are willing to put our life into Its hands and ask It to direct us. As soon as we do so, It will accelerate our past karma and help us to balance it. The High C will never give us more than we are able to bear at any time. We are always free to make a conscious decision to seek the help of the High C and co-operate with It. Or, we can refuse to seek Its guidance and continue to try to steer our own course until we founder and either ask for help or collapse.

If we want to, we can accelerate our evolution by trusting our High C to know what we lack. The so-called ordinary way of life, of reacting to whatever life throws at us would, of course, also lead us back to our source, but it is very slow. Without the guidance of the High C, we invariably try to evade the very lessons each life is designed to teach us. Whereas, with the High C in the pilot's seat, we are certain to pass through all the jumps and bumps and storms on our way and arrive in one piece!

There is a mantra which I have found very helpful in following this approach. It is, 'Surrender, trust and accept', that is, 'I surrender to the High C who knows best what I need; I trust It to bring about whatever that may be; and I will accept whatever may occur, whether I like it or not!'

With our very limited conscious view, we are not in a position to know what is best for us. The High C, knowing the past as well as the present, is better able to decide for us, if we grant It the authority to do so.

We too often limit our growth in one way or another for many different reasons: fear and timidity, low self-esteem, guilt or even laziness. If we repeatedly ask for what is right for us at the time, we will find we are given much more than we could possibly imagine or hope for. By removing the constricting layers we have accumulated over many lifetimes, we will automatically free ourselves to be consciously in touch with the High C and allow It to take over the direction of our lives towards at-onement with It. When the darkness caused by the many layers of conditioning is removed, The High C's inner light can shine forth and irradiate not only ourselves but everyone and everything It touches through us.

More advanced techniques will now be set forth to guide those who need help with steps along the inner path towards union with God, instead of the outer way leading to attachment to the material world.

Chapter 15

EARLY CONDITIONING

As I look back over the years, it is quite clear that the people with whom I work fall into two distinct categories: one group is composed of those who primarily need to be given tools to use to overcome their current difficulties and to make possible a more positive and harmonious way of life. The other group comprises those who, as well as seeking a more effective life-style, want to dedicate themselves to the goal of wholeness and eventual liberation from desire – that is to say, from the grip of worldliness. These last people are invariably born into families in which they feel alien, like the Ugly Duckling.

When I first meet someone who fits into the latter group, I explain that the experience of feeling like a stranger in the natal family offers great advantages. Those who feel this way are discouraged from relying on their family for support or security. Instead they are obliged to become self-reliant from an early age. This is an extremely hard and painful way to start out in life and many people lack the strength to survive unscathed. Even those who do are usually forced to seek help at particularly difficult periods of their lives. Such crises, however, provided they are handled properly, can serve as initiations along the way. Crises provide the necessary tension, or pain, to force people to move through and out of them into a new state of awareness. As a result, more energy is freed for use in future developments.

The original method of cutting ties needs to be expanded and adapted to the particular needs of such people. The sequence of steps varies to fit the individual's needs, particularly at the beginning of the process when the preparation for separation from the parents is being initiated. The spiritual, mental and emotional atmosphere of the home and the family background of both parents must be examined and understood to allow inherited patterns to be clearly revealed. These patterns often indicate the principal lessons to be learned by the person born into a particular family at this precise time. So, he needs to see them very clearly if he is to take advantage of the opportunity they offer for growth.

In order to obtain a clear view of the entire situation into which he is born, an individual must analyse everything to which he was exposed during his early years, whether the events or feelings were consciously or unconsciously experienced. He must observe in retrospect his reactions to many different influences, to determine whether he has accepted them or rejected and rebelled against them. As he studies his reactions, he should try to ascertain if he has learned from each experience or missed the opportunity to do so.

It is always helpful to ask, 'Did I get the point of this or that experience? What could it have taught me? Was I at a point in my development where I could learn from it? If not, has a similar experience recurred, and have I subsequently learned the lesson it held, or will it need to be repeated? If so, have I now gained sufficient insight to manage it positively the next time it occurs?'

I have learned from my own experience, and from working with others, that it is necessary to examine very carefully both the general and individual early influences. These include nationality, with the customs, beliefs, prejudices, attitudes, characteristics, food, superstitions and everything else connected to each different one. In addition, there are numerous other influences, such as the location where the family live, the social and financial background, level of education, range of interest in cultural subjects, sports, art, music, reading, gambling, drinking, partying and other activities. All these should be examined in order to assess the extent to which they have affected the person and how he has used, or wasted, the opportunities for growth which they provided.

He also needs to recognise how these early influences have affected his present behaviour. He may be quite unconscious of the ways in which he is still susceptible to them. Dreams are an invaluable aid in discovering unconscious influences. They will be discussed later.

I must issue a warning at this point, that scrutiny of early life is not intended to be the signal for criticising anyone or anything. The important point is not whether something or somebody was good or bad, but how the person under scrutiny reacted to them, and to what extent they coloured his present outlook.

To be completely free in the full sense of the word is to be detached from past influences and able therefore to extract the maximum benefit from the immediate present. In other words, it is best to remain free to use what is of value and discard what is worthless, rather than to be a pawn to either alternative.

Everything, even the seemingly negative experiences, can be used to further one's way towards the goal. No part of one's origins or early years need be wasted or viewed as disgraceful or mistaken if the learning it brought is accepted and used.

The lists of both parents' attributes, compiled at the time of cutting the ties to them, should be carefully examined for clues to help in discovering early programming. But, for this more detailed work, the list of influences must be greatly expanded and projected against the background of the family heritage to help a person to see the overall pattern to which he was exposed and to which he has reacted in his own way by complying, rebelling, or making some kind of adjustment or compromise.

The belief in the theory of reincarnation is very helpful in supplying possible reasons for a person's birth into a certain family. It can also indicate the lessons he needs to learn which his present environment makes possible.

It is sometimes essential to connect a person to the Cosmic Parents *before* he detaches himself from his physical ones. They can then supply him with the nourishment, security and acceptance he needs that his own parents, being human and therefore limited, were unable to provide to the required extent.

At birth, the spirit enters a new body in a new family and, in so doing, derives everything connected to it for many generations. The particular body is a container for the spirit for a relatively short time, more or less three-score years and ten, as the Bible says. All these influences have their effect for that lifetime, and will carry over into future lives, just as those of past lives have carried over into this one.

It seems that the spirit is drawn to enter a particular embryo according to its past karma. The new body and set of circumstances are those most suitable to enable it to work out or erase past mistakes, learn unfinished lessons, and generally reap the rewards or punishments of past acts. The saying, 'Whatsoever ye sow, so shall ye reap,' expresses this concept.

I shall never forget the profound relief I felt when I realised that I was not to blame for the problems my two daughters had inherited, such as allergies, if it was true that their heritage was chosen, or they were drawn to it because they needed to learn from the various problems inherent in it. The law of cause and effect never deviates. Whatever we have put into action in the past, we will experience either in this life or in a later one. We need always to ask what will further us on our inner path back to the Godhead and what will hinder our progress.

So, the baby at birth entering a new life via a new family will be affected or programmed not only by the people and events of this new life, but also by the patterns carried within itself from all its past lives. It does not arrive into the new body as a blank, ready to be imprinted by all it encounters this time. It has already been programmed by its entire past and contains within it, on an unconscious level, the memory of all it has experienced thus far, both in male and female bodies.

In order to break free of the wheel of birth, death and rebirth, we need to detach ourselves from all the many personalities we have assumed, the bodies we have inhabited and the desires we have felt over a vast span of time. We have all initiated many acts, some of kindness and some otherwise. These must be accounted for and balanced before we are free to make our return to the Godhead, unencumbered by the burden of all our past actions.

In each new life, as a member of a new family, we are given the very opportunities we need to balance our spiritual ledger and thus free ourselves for the return to our source: reunion with the High C and, simultaneously, with the universal God-force inherent in every living creature.

When examining the influences of the environment/external circumstances into which a soul is born, it is important to bear in mind that they can be likened to a school in which are taught the lessons that still need to be learned. The reaction to the various problems that occur is the most important consideration, not the hardships they apparently cause.

Each of us has had many lives in the past, all very different from one another. Each time we have re-entered the world, we have been attracted to it by those of our desires which attach us to the people, things and places we regard as indispensable to our fulfilment. If we can become desireless, we will discover that we have been freed from attachment to the world and its contents and can live in it but remain so unattached to it that it loses the power to lure us back into a new body.

Thus our whole environment can offer exactly what we need to become strong, wise, loving and unselfish, and to acquire many other positive traits we still need in order to become whole – for instance, the discrimination to distinguish between the things which come from truth, and that we can therefore accept, and those that are false and should therefore be rejected.

Since everything and everybody can be looked upon as a test, it is wise to ask, 'What can this particular experience, person or incident teach?' This simple question can prevent a lot of heartaches, rebellion and worry. But, for most of us, that is a very difficult attitude to attain and requires a great deal of practice, as it is often in direct opposition to all we have been taught.

Chapter 16

SYMBOLS

Symbols are used as a means of conveying certain messages to the subconscious mind in order to gain its co-operation in the self-integration process. Symbols provide an effective method of communication with that part of the mind because they are its natural language, a fact observable in dreams. This much will be familiar to those who have read my previous work.

In this more advanced work, symbols are even more important for correctly conveying subtler messages. A symbol is the container of a message, or, as is more often the case, a complex of several messages. The more a symbol is used, the more energy it accumulates from continuous and repeated usage. In this way, it beams the message inherent in a symbol more and more powerfully to the subconscious of those who are using it. Symbols can be likened to thought-forms filled with energy.

The same symbols can be used either constructively or destructively. In mass hypnosis, a symbol is used as the bearer of a concept which is then repeatedly projected, with strong feeling or emotional energy, to large groups of people. The effect of such a strong emotional impact on a crowd is well known. The people comprising the group lose their individuality and act as one unit, swayed by whoever is seeking to influence them. So a powerful message delivered by a charismatic authority-figure is able to reach directly to the subconscious.

Hitler is recognised as having effectively used negative mass hypnosis. He used an ancient symbol, the swastika, which, because of its long use, carried with it the energy accumulated over many centuries. But he used the anticlockwise version, associated with the negative or left-hand path of black magic including total control, as opposed to the positive, clockwise version which has a freeing, integrating and beneficial effect.

We are all influenced by symbols or thought-forms from birth to death. We are conscious of some of them but many are sent and received on the unconscious or subliminal level. The old saying, 'Thoughts are things,' expresses very succinctly the nature of a thought-form or symbol. It has a shape and is filled with energy. It is, therefore, a living form given energy by those who use it. Another saying, 'You are what you think,' also refers to the power of thought. However, it is not only what we think consciously, but what we accept on an unconscious level that affects our lives and behaviour.

Anything repeated regularly and with conviction, whether by thinking, saying, or acting, carries energy, whether it is projected consciously or subliminally. The latter way is more effective because the material received is not processed by the logical part of the brain. It is ingested without thought or choice. It is important to be free to question everything we take into ourselves before accepting it. We should not blindly accept everything.

But we are all influenced by persuasion in many different forms. As soon as we enter the world, we are immediately bombarded by all the customs, taboos, prejudices, fears, superstitions, beliefs and habits of the family we have entered. These are all thought-forms that contain the energy of those many many people who have accepted and used them and, in so doing, continued to add to their potency. Some of these thought-forms are timeless and still useful, others are outdated or inapplicable to our present life-styles.

We must determine if we are controlled by unsuitable patterns. If we are, then, to some extent, we are not free to express our true selves and are slaves to the symbols representing the customs or beliefs we hold to. If they are of a positive nature, enhance life and are in agreement with the High C's guidance, then we would be foolish to discard them. Obviously, we should not reject the valuable aspects of our heritage, but only those that enslave us or prevent us from being free to grow and to ask for guidance from the High C.

When we have detected an attitude, belief or habit that is affecting us adversely, we should look back to our childhood to discover its genesis. What oft-repeated inherited belief, theory, superstition or idea are we reacting to and repeating? As soon as that becomes clear, we must first find an appropriate symbol to express it. It is best to ask the High C to supply one. It may be in the form of an image, a memory, a thought or feeling, but it must have meaning to us personally so that there is an inner recognition when it is accurate.

That symbol should then be put in the opposite circle of the Figure Eight with the visualised blue neon light flowing around in the usual way, night and morning for two weeks. At the end of the fortnight, the control of the habit or activity expressed in the symbol will have lost much of its power and will be seen for what it was, master over us, its helpless slaves. With the newly acquired perspective, and the energy we had invested in it, and which gave it power over us, retrieved for our own use, we will discover that we are strong enough to make a decision to detach ourselves from its control. The detachment can be accomplished through a regular cutting where the symbol is perceived to be attached to a part of the body by a cord or other bond, or as a growth or excrescence. The help of the High C is essential to determine how it should be removed and destroyed, and how any remaining energy should be drawn out of it and brought back into us.

The most important part of this undertaking is to determine the correct symbol to represent the original thought-form, repeatedly projected until it became so deeply embedded in the subconscious that it expressed itself in automatic behavioural patterns.

But since we are all born into a family with everything that it involves, in accordance with the karma we have earned, each new birth offers a chance to learn whatever we have failed to learn in each past life. This learning is made possible by the very problems and frustrations we meet, particularly during our early years, for they give us the opportunity to experience for ourselves the pain we inflicted on others by some of our past actions.

But we are equipped with free will, so we can consciously decide not merely to learn from the problems we encounter, but also to try to bring about a better balance in our lives. The close relationships between ourselves and others in the family in which we are born provide the necessary means to do this.

By taking control of our karma, we can accelerate our release from it. That, in turn, hastens our freedom from the attachments that still hold us prisoners to our physical, mental and emotional desires. Obviously, we cannot erase the past since it has vanished. But we can and should live in the present and endeavour to surrender to the High C, thus incurring no further effects on our karma, either good or bad, to be absorbed and reabsorbed in future lives.

Chapter 17

DETACHING
OURSELVES FROM ROLES

By cutting ties to people, habits, inherited characteristics and all other outer controlling factors, we will be taking responsibility for our karma and conscientiously working to overcome it. This process involves self-scrutiny. That means repeatedly asking ourselves, 'Who am I?' We should check the multiple roles with which we identify ourselves and realise that to believe we are any of them prevents us from finding the answer to that question.

An alternative method for identifying the many and varied roles is to recognise that, 'I am not this one or that one.' As soon as a role becomes clear, an appropriate symbol to represent it can be visualised in the opposite circle of the Figure Eight. The exercise is practised for two minutes each morning and evening for two weeks.

Sometimes, this simple exercise is sufficient to release the control or domination of the role. If not, by consulting the High C, either on our own or with another person, a method will be shown whereby it can be destroyed. But the energy invested in it must first be withdrawn and reabsorbed into the person. The best way is to breathe in the energy and let go of any further attachment to the role by breathing it out.

In *Cutting the Ties that Bind*, many specific symbols and

techniques are given to help release people from their various controlling factors. In this book, relying on the High C to provide methods of release is advocated as it is preferable to using symbols suggested by someone else. In this way, it is possible to become less dependent on outer sources and more conscious of the promptings of the High C. Gradually, in the process of becoming free, we have to relate only to the High C's guidance. With daily practice, it becomes easier to receive intimations from that source.

The world is peopled by human beings, some functioning in male and some in female bodies. The union of the two is designed to produce new individuals, thus replenishing the population. But, the real Selves that reincarnate into the world as babies are neither exclusively male nor female but in essence both. In other lifetimes they have undoubtedly experienced living in male and female bodies. The varied experiences allowed them to accumulate the needs and knowledge each gender can provide.

It is the spirit resident in the body that is the true, permanent and indestructible Self. The physical form, male or female, is only a temporary vehicle through which the divine spirit manifests itself in the world. The eventual goal of each spirit is to merge into its own core. The soul has many facets or potentials which, when experienced in various lives, become conscious, bringing to consciousness what had hitherto been unconscious.

We carry on the unconscious level, as in a memory bank, all the attributes we have developed over many lifetimes. These are available to us at any time if we conscientiously work to raise them up to the conscious level where they can be used in our everyday life. However, we are not completely free to flower into our true potential in any of our lives, for many different influences have overlaid the original pattern in each lifetime, some beneficial to growth and others not. It is as if many coats, or shells, have been laid down, layer by layer, around the inner core, or spark of divinity, which is our essence. This makes it very difficult for us to keep close contact with the Self, or even to recognise its existence.

We need, first, to recognise these coverings and roles, and then, systematically remove them. That will allow the pure flame of the spirit to be revealed. It can then illuminate the physical sheaths of body, mind and emotion, and make them pristine pure, and be in complete control of all our activities all the time. We will eventually be able to live free from all outer influences and put into practice 'Thy will, not mine'. 'Thy will' refers to the will of the true Self, finally uncovered and given. Its rightful place as the controller in our lives. This is the ultimate goal of all human beings as they move forward through the centuries towards a reunion with the true Self – and therefore with all others for, at the High C level, we are all one.

This process is essentially a way to become fully conscious, for only when we are conscious of an attitude, weakness, role, or desire can we decide if we should let go of it or retain it, depending on whether it will advance or hinder our progress. To achieve this requires hard work, but to what better use can we put our lives than to clear a path back to union with our true Self?

This essential information is largely omitted from our education, especially in the West. As a result, we feel ill-equipped for the hard work this search entails. We have too few guidelines to direct us, so we become more and more entangled in the endless intricacies of our physical lives in the outer world. We either forget, or are unaware of, an inner path which can lead us back to our source by taking us from the human state to the divine, our unique birthright.

This process does not only sound like a huge undertaking, it is just that. It should be our life's work, but it does not have to be accomplished all at once. There is a sequence of steps that will eventually lead us out of our cages, or prisons, into the sunlight of the true freedom which is our real and divine condition.

Chapter 18

MEN
AND WOMEN

It is to be hoped that the confusion rampant in the world and the desperate need for guidelines to the roles of men and women will force us all to let go of the old concepts and allow the very necessary changes to take place. The education of children will need to be completely revised so that students of each sex may be encouraged to develop all their innate faculties and become whole and secure individuals, utilising both their male and female qualities in the right proportions.

At birth, a spirit, neither male nor female, but beyond both, takes up residence in a male or female body with all that each form signifies. From the beginning of time, there have been patterns of behaviour, customs and taboos for each sex. These vary from culture to culture, or for each group, into which a person is born. Some of these behaviour patterns are still applicable, while others are outmoded and no longer viable. We need, therefore, to discriminate between those that are no longer useful and those that will enable us to live our lives as men or women more fully. If the roles are too rigid they restrict freedom of development and prevent us from being free to turn within to the High C.

These original male and female roles are impressed on the child both consciously and on an unconscious level, first by the parents and then by the society into which it is born. Sometimes it is difficult to accept the male or female role. If one or both parents do not accept it, the task is made harder. Each sex offers different living experiences. When these are accepted, the soul gains; when they are rejected, it misses an opportunity to learn. However, a woman is not just a woman. A man is not just a man. Each possesses the attributes of both. The heart and the head, or yin and yang, both need to be expressed in each sex.

When we inhabit a female body or vehicle, feeling, heart, receptivity and compassion should be more dominant, with intellect, head, assertiveness and logic in supportive roles. For those who inhabit a male body, the reverse should be the aim. When there is inner balance between the two aspects, there is not such a feverish need to seek the contrasting characteristics in a person of the other sex. Alliances can then be maintained without the need for one partner either to dominate or be dominated by the other. Both can become more balanced by expressing both sides of their nature, rather than by living in a symbiotic relationship where each leans on the strong qualities of the other instead of developing their own weaker ones.

Men have, through the centuries, been educated to consider themselves the superior, or leading sex and have devalued not only women but also their own inner feminine nature. This has resulted in a kind of 'heart bypass' in the world. In a reverie, I was once shown superimposed over the earth a huge human figure with all the chakras clearly visible as whorls of energy. I was made aware that the heart chakra was almost completely cut off from the others and, therefore, from the flow of the universal life-force. This was true both at the world level as well as the individual personal level. It is very clear that the heart, or feminine aspect, has been suppressed at every level of society, for love and compassion seem to be absent and aggression and violence are becoming more and more frequent.

Men should not only think, analyse, rationalise and control, but should balance these qualities with empathy, consideration of others and genuine love. Likewise, women should bring into daily situations their ability to think in an organised way rather than relying on men to carry out this function for them, but this should not be at the expense of their feeling nature.

All four functions of intuition, sensation, intellect and emotion should be developed as much as possible in both sexes to bring about a more balanced and integrated person, whether male or female. The Mandala already described in detail can help with this balance.

Unfortunately, in the world today, there are very few role models of truly feminine women whose animus or yang side is a strong motivating force within them. There are also very few truly masculine men who are in contact with their inner anima or feeling nature. Many men scorn their feminine nature due, in part, to their conditioning as children. Many boys were taught that it is not manly to show feelings and that boys don't cry or they will be called sissies. But, when any part of a person is suppressed, it often erupts from the subconscious, where it has been imprisoned, in an effort to bring about balance. When this happens, it is usually out of control, and is expressed too strongly or violently, which can cause extreme embarrassment to the person involved.

Due to the centuries-old domination by masculine virtues, women often strive to imitate men and, in so doing, become pale carbon copies of them. But they then deny their own femininity, which should rightfully be their strongest function. So, instead of the world being brought back to a more balanced state after centuries of male supremacy, it is becoming even more confused, because both men and women are dominated by their masculine, or yang, nature at the expense of their hearts. But the constant movement in the cosmos towards balance must eventually succeed, however long it takes.

It is the individual and group attachment to one or other of any of the pairs of opposites that causes a state of imbalance and produces rigidity instead of flow. It is as if a pendulum had swung too far to one or other extreme and had stopped oscillating back and forth between the two poles.

Male and Female Roles

As soon as a child is born it is exposed to a whole heritage of beliefs, expectations and models of behaviour outlining its future role as a man or woman in the social milieu of the family. These patterns have been handed down through families from one generation to the next. Until fairly recently, family and ethnic groups tended to remain largely intact. Many nationalities took great pride in preserving the purity of their family lines, free from the influence of alien customs. This meant that a young couple about to marry would usually have inherited similar family patterns, some families insisting on it despite the wishes of the prospective bride or groom.

There were arranged marriages in the East and marriage brokers in the West, both designed for the purpose of finding a man and a woman with appropriate backgrounds for a suitable match. This, of course, meant that the mores of the national or religious group were common to both partners and were therefore reinforced and perpetuated in the union.

But with more widespread travel, especially since the advent of cars and air travel, multitudes of people are mixing with members of other cultures. Many unions are taking place between individuals from very different backgrounds. Obviously, this can create serious difficulties if conflicting customs and beliefs are rigidly adhered to by either partner.

At present, there are no adequate guidelines for the roles of men and women. The old ones are of little use in these rapidly changing times but, as yet, no new ones have taken their place.

It is necessary to consider basic human values and adapt the old roles to fit the contemporary world. The new models will need to be designed for the whole world since it is rapidly losing the previous fixed boundaries between national groups and their varied customs.

As conventional roles for men and women become obsolete, what will take their place? More and more, we find men and women working side by side, engaged in the same work. This situation could enable each to develop his or her natural abilities, but not to the exclusion of those qualities usually attributed to the other sex. Both men and women need to bring about a balance between head and heart within themselves so that each is able to feel as well as think.

Women in particular should not be made to feel inadequate if they do not fit the accepted model of their national group or family. For example, not all women fit the stereotype of a pretty, sexy blonde. Nor do all men fit the macho image so long over-emphasised. These roles, composed as they are of thought-forms, need to be changed so that members of each sex can be free to express their own unique attributes without being forced to fit a traditional role model.

Women will always be the ones to bear children, but that need not be their sole contribution to society. Likewise, the fact that men do not give birth to babies is no reason why they should not take part in the care and training of their children.

With so many women now going out to work, husbands are beginning to do their share of the household tasks. In this way the roles are becoming less separate and distinct. As parents co-operate in the care of their children, their example will condition the next generation along the new lines. They are pioneers, which is always a hard task.

The roles are at present in limbo, but they are on the way to assuming a new form to fit present-day needs. The ties to old useless moulds need to be cut to make room for the newly created ones that are slowly being revealed, for only if we cut away from the past can we move freely into the future.

One of the main causes of male chauvinism is the belief that mental and intellectual achievements are superior to all others. This idea appears to stem from the fact that the cultivation of the brain and its intellectual faculty is the most recent development in man's evolutionary journey from earliest primitive times to the present day. The result is a tendency to worship mental powers above and beyond the other three functions found in man – namely, sensation, emotion and intuition. But, all four are of equal importance and the development of each is necessary for eventual wholeness.

The function which has suffered most by being not merely neglected, but actually scorned, is that of feeling or emotion. It is the function through which love, compassion, empathy, mercy and other gentle, unselfish urges are expressed. These are being threatened with extinction at present, having been rejected in favour of intellectual prowess.

Accompanying the adulation of reason and the denigration of feeling is the chauvinistic attitude of many men towards women. Since superior intellectual ability has long been associated with men, it is understandable that they should consider themselves superior to women. The inevitable reaction to this artificial and erroneous concept is seen in the fairly recent strong rebellion of women against this unbalanced state of affairs.

Men and women are not identical. Each sex carries male and female attributes in different proportions and expresses them differently. Both men and women need to bring about a balance between the two poles of male–female, positive–negative, yang–yin within themselves. Both heart and head must be cultivated and given expression by both sexes. Neither is superior to the other. The two need to work in harmony to provide polarity and balance in the individual. This will allow both men and women to become clear channels through which the High C can guide them and eventually absorb the personality and ego into Itself to bring a return to the Godhead.

We each need to determine our own truth. We should not continue to be influenced by the narrow beliefs and superstitions that may be held by our parents and other members of the group into which we were born, or in which we are now living.

Superimposed over the original male and female roles are many variations which are quickly assumed as minor roles by the child. A child is born to two parents, but there are many other relationships already established in the family which will automatically create other roles for the newcomer from the very start of his or her life. These are considered below.

Son and Daughter

At birth, a baby is immediately either a son or a daughter with all the accumulated customs and patterns each carries with it. It immediately moves into one or other set of codes of behaviour which it will be expected to follow and which will mould its understanding and dictate its behaviour as it develops.

The role of a son or daughter should be temporary. If either is continued without change beyond the attainment of adulthood, an unhealthy dependence on one or both of the parents will result. In such cases, if the parents continue to retain their early authoritarian roles, the son or daughter will continue to act as a child and identify himself or herself with those early roles long after they themselves have become parents, or even grandparents. Only when the early roles of son or daughter are relinquished can a person move on to the more mature role of parenthood. Grown children who still act, think and feel like children are not fit to assume a strong parental role themselves. They are apt to compete with their own children instead of presenting role models for them. There are far too many cases of child-adults rearing children and automatically passing on this incorrect pattern to future generations.

After cutting the ties to each of the parents, it is usually sufficient to practise the Figure Eight with a symbol of the son or daughter role in the opposite circle. However, at the end of the two-week practice period, the circle containing the old role may be separated and pushed off into outer space, into a volcano, or otherwise disposed of. If the role has been retained too long, it may even be necessary to perform a ritual to complete the detachment. The High C can be asked to indicate the best method. The person can then be free to assume the role whenever appropriate, but they need not be so completely identified with it that they helplessly continue to play it when it is inappropriate.

Brother and Sister

In addition to the role of son or daughter, those of a brother or a sister may be assumed at birth. These relationships can be close and compatible or highly competitive and antagonistic, depending on many factors. Sometimes karmic patterns may be in operation, in which case the present relationship offers an opportunity to balance out old debts or differences and, in so doing, gain the necessary experiences.

Groups of souls sometimes incarnate at the same time for their reciprocal learning. This situation can bring with it problems involving the present relationships unless the previous ones have been released. For instance, a mother may at some time have been a brother, sister, husband, wife or child to her present child. If the former relationship was emotionally charged, it can overshadow the present one with confusing and sometimes disastrous results.

At the same time, it becomes obvious that no one particular person is our only sister, mother, child or other relative. Only for each lifetime is a relationship valid. As Baba tells us, 'Every man is your brother, every woman is your sister and every child is your child; all are members of the human family.'

A clarification of the various roles, and detachment from them, alleviates a great deal of the confusion that is so evident in relationships between people. This present life is the only one that should concern us. We can learn and grow only in the here and now. The past is gone and no longer in our power to change. The future is unknown, being still in the making, our own making, as we conscientiously live in the present as wisely and lovingly as possible by asking for guidance from the High C.

Grandson and Grand-daughter

The roles of grandson and grand-daughter are two more roles automatically assumed at birth, whether all four grandparents are alive or deceased. These also need to be released to allow the grandchild to become an independent adult, with the High C as its sole authority.

Grandparents can be of tremendous help to a child by giving the love and attention they now have the time to bestow. But, to remain dependent on them indefinitely limits a child's growth and freedom to express its own potential. When a grandchild becomes an adult, respect can still be shown to the grandparents. But it is imperative to remain steadfast in following the inner guidance of the High C, and to resist any coercion from the grandparents to do their bidding if it conflicts with an inner conviction.

Again, as in the relationship with parents, a grandchild's true identity and worth do not depend on the fame, fortune, or prowess of the grandparents. He has his own path to tread, with all the challenges it brings along the way. To live in the shadow or reflection of famous parents, grandparents or other relatives can hamper a person's own growth as well as threaten his self-confidence. Each person has his own destiny and should live accordingly. He cannot assume anyone else's or have others assume his. So it is advisable to practise the Figure Eight with the role of grandchild in the opposite circle, as with other roles.

Mother and Father

It is advisable not only to cut the ties to parents but, in addition, for parents to cut the ties to their children after they have attained maturity. This ritual sets both parents and grown children free to interact as independent adults. The parents, having reared their children as well as they were able during the early years of their growth and development, can hand them over to the High C to guide them from then on. Then the children are also free to develop into mature adults independent of their parents and under the direct guidance of the High C.

When the ritual cutting is undertaken by both parents and children, the subconscious mind of each receives a very strong symbolic message, which enables it to help them all put into practice the freedom to live from then on as separate individuals. There is then far less danger of parents continuing to act as authority-figures. Parents who try to control their children after they have reached adulthood are not being as kind and loving to them as they may believe; quite the reverse, for they are actively hampering their children's growth and delaying their independence.

There is another step in this emancipating process. It involves the willingness of the parents of grown children to cut the ties to the parental role so that they will not be tempted to enact it indefinitely. Parents and their grown children can then interact as equals, as with other adults.

Grandparents

Following parenthood, the roles of grandmother and grandfather may be assumed and, eventually, need to be released, for they, too, should be helpful and not dominating. Sometimes, in a family, grandparents represent even more of an authority than the parents, in which case there is a wider generation gap separating the current way of life from their own and one which is likely to be outmoded and no longer practicable. A clash of wills between parents and grandparents can easily ensue, with the children caught in the middle of the conflict.

Of course, whenever possible, it is preferable for a harmonious connection to exist between the generations. In the West, where families are usually separated from other members by custom or distance, children are deprived of the support and love of an extended family. Grandparents have usually retired from active life and have more time to devote to their grandchildren than they had for their own children. They can also supply their grandchildren with the added source of wisdom and love from their own longer experience.

However, they may have remained so attached to their role of authoritative parents that they merely add to its dimension the role of grandparents and continue to be controlling rather than supportive. They need to cut away from both roles, which would allow them the freedom to make a very important contribution to their grandchildren's development.

Often a person will mention that the relationship with a grandparent was the only source of love and understanding available to him during childhood. The love and acceptance of just one person can provide a child with the security and sense of self-worth he so desperately needs to develop into an independent and healthy adult.

Other Roles

There are also other peripheral roles, such as nephew, niece and cousin, which may also need to be released, depending on the intensity of the attachment.

As the child matures and leaves the family home to start a new family, he is likely to acquire additional roles: husband or wife, father or mother, aunt or uncle and, eventually, grandfather or grandmother. He needs to be detached from all these roles since none of them is his true identity.

Chapter 19

BALLOON AND
NEST-OF-DOLLS ROLES

In addition to the roles determined by the various relationships to other members of the family at birth, there are two separate and distinct roles that start to develop very early in life. One, the Balloon, is initiated by the baby himself. The other, the Nest of Dolls, is projected on to the growing child by its parents or other members of the family. They both usually continue throughout childhood and can become a part of the adult.

These two early roles set patterns of behaviour that lead directly to other roles that may be assumed later in life.

The Balloon

As soon as a baby is born and takes its place in the family, it instinctively learns how to achieve its primary needs of food, security, acceptance and love.

It is fascinating to watch very tiny babies try out different ploys to gain the attention of their parents and other family members to get what they want. Depending primarily on the reaction of the parents or other guardians, they soon start to play a particular role or roles that appear, from their limited experience, to enable them to satisfy their needs and, at the same time, discover their niche in the family.

Parents seem rarely able to accept a child's true identity or allow him to unfold like a flower by watering him with their love and care. They invariably have preconceived ideas of what he should be like, which is usually either their idea of perfection or a carbon copy of themselves or both!

Many parents consider their children to be extensions of themselves and expect them to present to the world a perfect image that will enhance their own worth in the eyes of their relatives, friends and acquaintances, as also the rest of the world.

As children are primarily intent on self-protection, they instinctively assume the roles most likely to provide them with the security they need. Their assumed roles become like rafts, security blankets, or armour to protect their sensitive, newly developing personality. An early role will be adapted and enlarged as the need arises or as the family situation changes.

The chosen role can be that of a people-pleaser, if the child senses that he will get what he wants only by complying with the wishes of his parents and others. If the parents' attention can be obtained only when the child is naughty, and is forthcoming only in the form of punishment or criticism, he quickly realises that if he plays the role of the bad child, he will force the parents to notice him. There is also the role of the rebellious child who soon picks up the message that he will gain attention if he has a tantrum or defies his parents. Even though the result of both the last two roles is pain of some kind, that is evidently preferable to indifference.

Other children discover that they will be praised if they are clever at school or good at some activity such as a sport, music, art or acting. In such cases, they will become over-achievers in an effort to gain the praise they crave.

If a child discovers that there is no way he can elicit the care and attention he needs, he withdraws within himself as a form of self-protection and escapes from participation in situations where he feels he has no real part to play. He lives his own private life deep within himself and away from his seemingly insensitive parents. This role, which is really an absence of any role, is much more difficult to drop. It often takes many years before the necessary courage is developed allowing the person to come out of the comparative safety of his protective shell. But the resulting freedom is always well worth the effort.

There are many other roles assumed by children at a very early age, influenced by the situation in which they find themselves at birth. Sometimes a role is programmed into the child even before birth. For instance, a child may be conceived in the hope of reuniting the two parents after a separation or rift in their relationship has occurred. The baby enters the family with that thought-form already in its consciousness and proceeds to live out the expectations imposed on him by taking on the role of conciliator.

It is easy to see that a mask, or role, was originally assumed as the most useful device for coping with the circumstances in which a child found himself at birth. But it is no longer necessary or useful after the child has attained maturity. It should be discarded after the ties to both parents have been cut. If it is continued too far beyond that age, it tends to become permanent and the person continues to play the once useful role in situations where it is inappropriate.

A role is like any habit which has been consistently repeated over a long period of time. It becomes very strong, being fed with the person's very breath, or life-force. He uses his energy to play the chosen role, often to the point of identifying himself with it so completely that he believes it to be his real self. It was originally a well-trained servant attending to his master, but it can turn into a parasite living off its host. The roles are then reversed: the servant becomes the master and the master is reduced to slavery. The role has become more powerful than its creator and eventually overwhelms him.

When such a condition exists, the person needs to find security in the High C, so that he may have the confidence required to discard the role. The Tree technique, as outlined in *Cutting the Ties that Bind*, is an excellent method for providing the necessary security from the two Cosmic Parents who together form the High C.

Most people find it comparatively easy to identify the main role they assumed in childhood. Often a person is acutely aware of behaving inappropriately in circumstances where the role is not called for. But, because it is stronger than him, he is powerless either to control or change it. He may realise, for instance, that he acts in all situations as a people-pleaser, or is unnecessarily belligerent, or must always appear perfect or some other quality, but is helpless to detach himself from the assumed role.

Some people are so completely submerged in their role that they have difficulty recognising it. It is helpful to suggest to such people that they allow their mind to travel back to childhood. That may help to determine the circumstances that prompted them to assume a particular role. Usually the nature of it will then begin to become clear. Other members of the family can also be most helpful in identifying it. They may remark that so and so was always the clever one, or the helpful one, or the funny one in the family. The wide variety of roles that are assumed by children to help them handle early situations is extraordinary. Their innate instinct to survive at any cost prevails, even at the expense of their identity.

The symbol that presented itself to designate this self-initiated role is that of a balloon which has been gradually inflated with the breath of the person during childhood and has continued unabated into adulthood. It is like one of those giant balloons with a face painted on it, seen at fairs, processions and amusement parks.

As preparation for detaching from this self-imposed role, a person is asked to visualise a large balloon projected out in front of his body and attached to it at some point by a cord or tube. Some people discover that they have more than one role, in which case they can visualise different faces on the surface of the balloon or several smaller balloons attached to the main one. They can usually name the various faces according to the roles they portray and some artistic people like to draw them. One young artist, who had been farmed out to many different families as a child, was forced to assume a different role in each family situation. She found great release in drawing and painting her image of each of the roles she had played.

As soon as a role has been identified, it needs to be placed in the opposite circle of the Figure Eight, to separate it from its creator, prevent any further control and allow for a clearer perspective of its effect on his life. At the end of the usual two-week practice period, he can arrange to meet a helper to complete the detachment. However, in many cases it can be achieved alone.

As the balloon is gradually created over a span of many years, it contains a large amount of its creator's energy, for it requires a great deal more energy to keep playing a role than to express one's true personality. The energy, *prāna* or *chi*, contained in the balloon symbol, needs to be reabsorbed or breathed back into its creator for use in more practical and constructive ways. To deflate it, the person who created it needs to imagine or visualise it projecting out in front of him, attached to his body at one or more points. He can then place his hands on either side of it, and squeeze out a little of the air it contains and inhale it back into himself. As he exhales, he should stop squeezing it and with a sigh, let go of any further need for it. This process should continue until the balloon is deflated and all that remains is a tiny, limp empty balloon. The old role is now devoid of its power to control him.

He should then ask his High C to indicate in some way the method best suited to destroy the remaining collapsed form. Some people are instructed to burn it, some drop it in an imaginary bowl of acid, some bury it, others cut it into a thousand pieces, or use many diverse methods to dispense with it. The circle in which it was first visualised as part of the Figure Eight is then erased. Finally, the person is directed to thank the High C, or real Self, for Its help and ask to be filled with Its energy and love to prevent the formation of any other false roles.

This method has proved to be most effective in removing from a person a whole pattern of limiting attitudes and allowing him to uncover a little more of his true nature.

The Nest of Dolls

The second of the roles that originates at a very early age is symbolised by a nest of dolls (often called 'Russian dolls') in which several dolls of graduated sizes are contained one within the other. As with most of the other techniques we have been given, this one was called forth in the course of my practical work. A young woman with whom I had been working for quite some time arrived with a problem that she was ready to address. She explained that she had recently become aware that although she was very successful in her work, she never really felt this to be true. Nor, for that matter, did she feel that she actually deserved to be successful, so low was her self-esteem. She had no clue to the underlying reason for this seemingly contradictory situation. I suggested she set aside a time when she could be free from distractions and allow her mind to travel back over her childhood. She could ask the High C to show her if the pattern originated in this lifetime, or was due to an overshadowing memory from a former life. I also proposed that she ask for a dream to indicate where this pattern could have started.

She returned several days later, having done her homework. As soon as she started to look at her problem more carefully, she realised that her brother suffered from a different version of the same basic problem. That insight led her to examine their family background in an effort to discover what had caused them both to feel so unworthy despite their respective successes. She had apparently blocked out from her memory the root cause and found it extremely difficult to uncover. Not until she felt more secure with her connection to the High C could she summon up enough interest and energy to do something about this condition. Slowly but surely, the pieces began to fall into place as she traced the following story.

Her mother was born to her grandparents several years after the birth of their first child, a daughter whom they adored. The second child was an accident and not welcome. They would have preferred to lavish all their love and attention solely on their firstborn. From the very beginning, they compared the two girls to each other and always with the same comments/results: that the second daughter would never be as pretty, as clever, as popular or as successful as her elder sister, she should not expect to marry as well, and so on. This programming was repeated throughout her childhood and beyond. She was influenced by it so thoroughly that she was not in any way as successful as her sister, did not marry as well and did not live in as nice a neighbourhood or in as large a house – all exactly as she had been programmed by her parents to expect.

She had believed and acted on this programming so completely that she continued to keep it alive by projecting it onto her own two children. She parroted her mother, who also repeated it to these two grandchildren, just as she had to their mother. She repeatedly told them they could never be as clever, attractive, successful or popular as their cousins. Their cousins, of course, had been assured by their mother, the adored child of the grandparents, that they were very special in every way, just as she had been raised to believe.

The result was a low self-image, despite the obvious fact that she and her brother had both worked hard to overcome it. Such repeated assumptions over many years lays down such patterns at a very deep subconscious level. Unless they are reversed, they will continue to dictate the attitudes and beliefs of the person so programmed.

Now that this young woman had uncovered the cause, what could be done to release her from this crippling pattern? It had no basis in truth and had forced her to be an over-achiever, yet never allowed her the relief that a sense of her own worth would have given her. Worse still, it made her feel that any success she did achieve was undeserved.

While she was talking, a strange image kept coming into my mind which seemed to have nothing to do with her account. It was a nest of Russian dolls. The large outer one contained graduated replicas, all identical except for size, ending with a tiny one. As I described the image, she gasped, and said, 'But that is exactly how I feel all the time, like a peasant who should not expect a better lot in life! And I feel guilty when I aspire to anything better.'

As we discussed the symbol, we saw how very appropriate it was. Deep inside all the others was the tiny doll with the larger ones forming layers or coverings around it, creating a kind of prison. That is precisely what had happened to her and her brother. Over the original little babies, layer after layer of identical conditioning had been laid down by the repeated words and condescending attitudes of their mother and grandmother. Understandably, they had both lived out the projected messages just as their mother and aunt had done before them.

She visualised the Nest of Dolls in the opposite circle of the Figure Eight with the blue neon light moving around it, every morning and night for two weeks. During that period, many forgotten and suppressed memories started to emerge from her subconscious where they had been hidden for so long. This showed once again how the Figure Eight gives perspective and separation so that a condition can be seen more clearly.

When she came back to work, and sought direction from the High C, she was shown a hammer and knew she must smash the outer layers of the hollow dolls one by one until she was left with the innermost minute but solid doll. She thoroughly enjoyed this imaginary activity, all the more so when she recalled the misery this projected image had caused her. After she had given full vent to her feelings by smashing all the hollow outer dolls, she gathered all the pieces and put them into a fire and watched as they were reduced to ashes. When I asked what whe would do with the ashes, she replied that she would gather them up and throw them into the ocean, which she then did. Next, I asked what she thought she should do with the tiny innermost doll. She described it as a kind of seed or tiny embryo, out of which she felt her new self could develop. I persisted in asking what she should do with it. After a long silence, in a little awestruck voice she said, 'Oh, I am to swallow it so that it can grow inside me,' and promptly did so.

However, it must be understood that it takes time for a new concept to take root as the old patterns begin to fall away, for these habits have been in control for so many years. Occasionally, the effect of such a session produces an immediate result but, more often, it takes time, though not nearly as long as it took for the role to be formed in the first place.

When such patterns, as symbolised by the Nest of Dolls, are continuously projected onto a developing child by an authority-figure, generally parent or teacher, as an adult he will expect all authority-figures throughout his life to repeat the early conditioning. If they do not express the same assumptions, he may even demand that they repeat his childhood programming.

To end this reaction, it is necessary to practise the Figure Eight exercise with a symbol for a typical authority-figure in the opposite circle. After two weeks a person can detach himself from the symbol in whichever way he is directed by the High C, to free him from domination by anyone who appears to be stronger or more impressive.

Children tend to consider their parents infallible, and, as a result, they firmly believe whatever they tell them until they discover, to their initial disbelief, that they are not necessarily always right.

A perfect example of this was a 6-year-old boy. While he was taking a shower one evening, his elder sister entered the bathroom. Seeing some round red blotches on his back and knowing that chickenpox had broken out in their school, she said, while pointing them out to him, 'Look! You have chickenpox.' He stoutly and angrily disagreed. So she called their father to come and look at them. He said they looked more like mosquito bites to him. Triumphantly, the boy said, 'See, Daddy says I haven't got chickenpox so I haven't and that's final!'

As soon as their grandmother arrived next morning to take them to school his sister, despite his angry protest, repeated that he had chickenpox. Their grandmother examined him and said it certainly did look like chickenpox to her. She suggested that the school nurse was the one who would really know, so they would go to school and ask her opinion. The nurse confirmed that it was, indeed, chickenpox and sent him back home. This was his first experience of discovering that his father could be wrong and he was devastated.

This little episode illustrates what a profound impression a parent's opinion has on a small child. Parents, being so much bigger and wiser, represent the ultimate authority until proved fallible. Depending on the way a parent uses authority, the child, as he matures, may fear or be in awe of all other authority-figures unless he has learned that they are not infallible. He may also find that he is repeatedly thrown together with people who are similar to his parents and, frustratedly, finds himself reacting to them as he did to his parents.

As so often happens in this work, the very next day after the Nest-of-Dolls symbol appeared, another woman came to work with me. As soon as she sat down, she burst forth with an account of her frustration, stemming from a very similar problem to the one brought by the first woman the day before. I started to outline the technique I had received. As I described the Nest of Dolls, she shot out of her chair in obvious disbelief. She proceeded to tell me that she had very recently given just such a toy to a child to play with. It had been given to her at her birthday party several years earlier, but she could never discover who had given it to her. Even stranger was the fact that within the last two weeks she had searched for the toy when her current boyfriend brought his young son to visit her. She wanted to find something to amuse the child and remembered she had put the Nest of Dolls away in a cupboard after the birthday party.

Now it was going to be put to a very different use to help her dispense with her low self-image. I instructed her to visualise the Figure Eight with the Nest of Dolls in the circle opposite her own. She left, delighted to have a tool with which to free herself from such a paralysing behaviour pattern. A few days later, I received in the post a package containing the Nest of Dolls she had been given. In her note she asked me to use it to help anyone else who might need the symbol to be rid of a similar problem.

The Hour Glass

After the Nest of Dolls has been destroyed, old inhibiting patterns often persist and prevent a person from being open to a more expansive life style.

Furthermore, many people have been taught a kind of reverse snobbery. Unlike children who received the message that they must keep up with the Jones, others were cautioned by their parents to know their place and not to try to emulate their superiors or more successful people.

In addition, many people limit themselves by insisting on having what they want or think is good for them instead of asking to be given whatever the High C knows they need. I have found that such insistence has a limiting effect, whereas, when we surrender to the High C and ask It to give us what we really need, we often receive far more than we could ever have imagined.

A symbol that can help to mitigate such limiting influences is the Hour Glass.

There are two ways to use the Hour Glass. To practise it alone, a gold circle delineating the personal space or territory is visualised at arm's length on the ground around the person. Then, instead of pulling it up to form the Cylinder it is pulled up to form a cone. The point at the top of the cone represents the High C, like the High C at the apex of the Triangle. Up above this basic cone, another inverted cone is visualized with the point of each cone just touching to form the neck of an hourglass with the upper cone open to the universe.

The other, even more effective way to set it up is to erect a Triangle with a partner, either present or at a distance. In this case the lower cone is visualized built up around the base line of the Triangle, with the Triangle filled out to form a cone. The upper cone is then visualized as before, open to the sky.

This method uses the natural polarity of the two people as with the Triangle, with each asking to be given what they need.

The person wishing to extend his limited horizons asks the High C to bring from the universe into the upper cone whatever is needed in the specific situation for which help is being sought. This then flows down, filtered through the High C at the neck of the Hour Glass, to the person in the lower cone, in the right amount and at the right speed and time.

The Hour Glass can be used for such specific requests as an appropriate job, a new house, a mate, clients, patients, customers and a host of other needs.

By opening up the situation under consideration in this way, and asking the High C to bring from the entire universe whatever is needed, previous old and limiting patterns can be overthrown.

Chapter 20

THE EFFECT OF ROLES
ON FUTURE RELATIONSHIPS

The Balloon and Nest of Dolls and other roles, or masks, if continued beyond their original need and usefulness, can cause serious problems later in life, particularly in close relationships such as marriage and friendships, business or professional partnerships, and with relatives.

There is a tendency to bring to other relationships the roles that were assumed in childhood. When two people form a close relationship, these roles often fit into one another, like a key in a lock. The outcome is apt to be ineffective communication, stultified individual growth, and other serious problems between the two partners. Frequently, when these roles are discarded, the two people concerned are able to form a different and more satisfactory relationship.

One of the most difficult patterns, and one which can play havoc in any relationship, is that of the 'rejected child'. No matter how accepting the partner may be, the rejected one will seek rejection, that being the only role he knows how to play, since it is a familiar one.

Another role that causes difficulties in a partnership is the 'people-pleaser'. These individuals never express their own wishes. They always wait until they hear what the other person wants so that they can then follow on and please the partner as they were conditioned to please the parent as children. These people will invariably form a relationship with a seemingly strong and controlling person whom they can follow, even though they may later rebel against the very situation they have actually brought about because it was familiar to them.

Yet another role that causes untold misery to whoever links their life to the one who plays it is the person who is always right and insists on doing or having only what he wants. They are the ones who were spoiled and indulged in childhood and have become monster-like in their demands. This type usually attracts someone who has had to cater to demanding parents. The two roles thus intertwine. But, after a while, intense stress develops in the slave-like one who then rebels against or vents his suppressed anger on his partner in subtle ways.

The list of roles is endless. Everyone can begin to catch sight of his own role or roles, as well as those of a partner. As soon as they are glimpsed, great understanding of the problems in the relationship will begin to dawn. When that happens, if they each use the Figure Eight and discard the roles, a better balance can be brought about. Both partners will be better able to express their true natures and, at the same time, respect one another's. Then a real companionship can begin to grow between them.

As an example, one couple consulted me because their marriage had reached an impasse. On questioning them, I discovered that the wife had experienced rejection even before she was born. Consequently, she continued to expect the pattern with which her developing consciousness had been imprinted. She had carried it to such lengths that she literally demanded rejection from others. Inevitably, her behaviour attracted rejection to her time and time again, even when others had originally intended to accept her.

Her husband played a very different role as a child. He was the only child of a very domineering mother. The only role available to him was to be subservient, programmed from his very first years to suppress his own opinions, desires and personality and to become a follower. His wife had appeared to be strong and independent, someone he could follow, thus continuing his early behaviour. But she only *seemed* to be strong. What appeared to be her fierce independence was really her need to be rejected. These two married and brought with them into the relationship their two individual patterns of behaviour. However, neither of them was aware of this situation, so each continued to play the adopted role until, eventually, they reached an impasse.

As soon as they realised what they had been unconsciously doing, they understood the problem they were creating between them. This insight in itself was a great relief, for conscious understanding of the cause brings hope of a solution. As long as they remained unaware of their separate roles, they were utterly frustrated, each blaming the other for the failure of their relationship.

It is always so much easier to see the faults of others and to be blind to our own. But we cannot possibly bring about a change in anyone else. Even if we point out a person's mistakes, if he is completely ignorant of them, it will be to no avail. We can only accomplish a change in ourselves, and then only if we ask the High C to help and are sufficiently disciplined to practise the various methods which will secure our freedom.

In a crisis like the one described above, both partners can ask the High C to present to their minds a suitable symbol to represent their separate roles. A symbol of the role can then be visualised in the other circle of the Figure Eight, with the blue neon light flowing around, for the usual two-week period, morning and night. At the end of that time, they should ask to be shown how to detach themselves from the roles. Various methods have been forthcoming. Sometimes, if the role has not become a deeply ingrained habit, it is sufficient to practise the Figure Eight to stop its control or identification with it. However, it is similar to all the other unnecessary blocks that prevent a person from receiving guidance from the High C and, like all thought-forms, it contains a person's energy. Since energy is neutral, neither positive nor negative, it should be re-absorbed by the person who launched it forth, clothed in the form of the role, so that it can be made available for positive use. There are many different ways to retrieve such energy for use in a beneficial way. Using the breath is the simplest way and usually brings the best result. Breathing is essential to life and is automatic and continuous, yet it is possible to assume conscious control of it. So, the energy a person has invested in the role is breathed back into himself and, as he breathes out, he can let go of any further need for it to continue to control him. As soon as the form of the role is destroyed and the energy returned to its source, the circle that contained it can be erased, or separated and pushed off into space.

If both members of a partnership are willing to destroy the roles they assumed in childhood, there is always the possibility that they will be free to relate to one another in a more realistic way, instead of through their roles. A more satisfying partnership often results, especially if they are both willing to consult the High C via the Triangle and request Its help in this task.

There are innumerable other combinations of early roles that lead couples into an eventual crisis accompanied by frustration, paralysis and depletion of energy. Alliances based on the mutual attraction of roles do not necessarily involve the real people hidden behind them. The roles have become habitual and, like all habits, are extremely hard to break or change. The longer they have been reinforced by practice, the harder it is to detach oneself from their hold. Only when the situation becomes intolerable, or threatens the well-being of one or both partners, will they be forced to make a change and attempt to break free from their condition. Desperation, extreme discomfort, resentment or frustration appear to be some of the necessary goads to galvanise people into initiating whatever action is needed to achieve a change.

However, a complete change can only be brought about by reprogramming the subconscious with the use of symbols that will correctly and simply convey a message directing it to achieve the desired changes. But even this method may fail if the habit is too strong or deep-seated. Some habits can only be broken with the help of the superior power of the High C. With Its help, major changes can occur, especially when both partners are willing to enlist Its aid. With our limited conscious minds, we can do very little to break free from old constricting patterns, but with the co-operation of the subconscious and the help of the superconscious, or High C, apparent miracles can be wrought, even in seemingly hopeless situations. But we do have, as our birthright, free will. That means that we can, with our conscious mind, continue to try to use its relatively inferior power to solve the problems, or capitulate and seek the help of the High C. When we willingly combine regular practice of the appropriate techniques to impress the subconscious and, at the same time, request the High C to help bring about whatever It knows we need, we are well on our way out of the morass and can begin to flow rather than stumble along our inner path. Then our life will be lived through us by the High C, instead of by us and we will incur no further karma.

In this way, growth and development can take place rather than continued stagnation leading inexorably to a living death.

A very common reaction of either or both partners in a close relationship is to try to elicit from the other whatever they have grown accustomed to expect from a parent. But, at the same time, great resentment is frequently felt when they receive the very reaction they sought or invited. Then the old frustration at the way they were treated by a parent is projected onto the partner. The end result is that they start to hate one another just as each had unconsciously, and sometimes consciously, hated the parent. But hatred of a parent is usually attended by feelings of guilt, so it is easier to hate the partner.

As soon as the origins and underlying reasons for the roles have become clear, they can be withdrawn and dealt with by each partner. It is then possible to replace the previous dislike, resentment or hatred with true gratitude for the understanding made possible.

It is perfectly legitimate to play a role when the occasion demands, but it should not be permanent or exclude the use of other more appropriate roles. It is the identification with a role, or the control it has gained over the person, that damages.

There is an old saying that it is impossible to teach an old dog new tricks, and there is some truth in this. If older people have become stuck in their old patterns and have not remained open to learning from new experiences, it may be too disrupting for them to break out of their moulds, especially if they have identified themselves too strongly with them. For that reason, Baba urges his devotees to concentrate on teaching children since they are so much freer and more adaptable, having had as yet little time to develop deeply ingrained habits. In addition, children are usually still closely in touch with the High C.

So, to summarise, first the early roles or strong habits have to be determined. Next, a symbol has to be found to contain the meaning so that the subconscious can comprehend the message and help to bring about a change. Then, to break the control the habit has assumed over the person, the Figure Eight is practised for at least two weeks depending on the strength and length of duration of the role. Lastly, a method has to be sought from the High C to destroy the symbol that represents the old pattern.

Two examples of roles from my own life illustrate their effect in more detail. I was born the only child of an extremely domineering and matriarchal mother and a gentle and kind father who was away from home a great deal due to his work. My mother was so fearful that I would become the proverbial spoiled only child that she resolved from the beginning to prevent that by being a strict disciplinarian. Because my father would have been more than likely to indulge me, she kept us apart even more than his travels did. The obvious outcome was that she was in almost sole charge of my up-bringing.

Apparently, this was the situation into which I needed to be born to help me to learn some of this life's lessons. But I also needed to fit into it in some way to find the security that all babies need from birth. I learned very early that, to avoid my mother's quick and violent temper, I must be neither seen nor heard any more than was absolutely necessary. I had to assume the role of the good and obedient child who was expected to do, feel, think and speak exactly as the mother demanded. I also had to adhere without fail to her rules, which were not only beyond my understanding, but not always even explained to me. I have been told by other relatives that my original nature was happy and free, but I soon learned that any form of free expression on my part only brought increased punishment. So I withdrew, in a desperate attempt to protect myself from my mother's control. Outwardly I was obedient, quiet, studious and helpful, but extremely serious, shy and repressed. Inwardly, I was imaginative, sensitive, artistically creative, extremely insecure and very lonely. As I look back, I realise that it was like putting a tightly fitting lid over a growing plant.

Another pattern my mother consistently projected onto me was symbolised by the way she used to introduce me to her friends as 'my weed'. It began when I grew very tall for my age, as well as woefully thin, which was her ostensible reason for choosing that particular appellation. Added to that, in self-defence, I always presented a seemingly imperturbable and unruffled demeanour which infuriated her. She did not feel she really controlled me unless I reacted violently, as she did. So she would sarcastically refer to me as always being as 'cool as a cucumber'. Weed and cucumber were combined in my opinion of myself, not surprisingly.

She herself was an ardent gardener who waged war on the detested weeds that threatened to choke her cherished flowers. And yet, she despised the daily task of uprooting them. So, to me, a weed was an inferior and unwanted species. That meant that, since it was my label, I too must be inferior and unwanted. Naturally, I had a very low self-image yet was expected to excel in every way so that the success would reflect on her and enhance her own image as the perfect mother.

Until this work started to take shape, I could find no way to break through the outer shell I had erected as a protection from my mother's control and conditioning. So I continued to be retiring, withdrawn, quiet and repressed. My balloon, or mask, which had started out as a protection, became my habitual attitude. Not until I was shown how to remove it was I able to allow my real personality to emerge and, eventually, be sufficiently free to express myself more confidently.

The knowledge that the true Self within everyone is of the same essence as the universal God-force also finally penetrated my protective armour. Oddly enough, simultaneously, I was able to gain a little much-needed weight once I no longer thought of myself as a weed.

I must not fail to mention that Baba has been responsible for giving me the courage to come out of my shell and to have made me willing to participate in the life of the world. I shall always be immeasurably grateful to him for his encouragement, reassurance and loving concern. He provided me with the love my mother was afraid to give me for fear of spoiling me.

Chapter 21

IDENTIFICATION WITH OCCUPATION OR PROFESSION

Some of the hats people wear are connected to their work. When asked to identify someone, a person will often answer that he is a plumber, a doctor, a labourer, a professor or of another occupation. That reduces the individual to the role his work occupies; however, he is not just that role but a lot more (besides.)

Unfortunately, many people define themselves according to the main role they play in life, or what they do everyday to earn a living, and fail to develop a well-rounded personality. Some people actually lose their identity beneath the weight of their job if it controls them instead of themselves being in control of their work.

The yoke should sit lightly on our shoulders rather than bending us to the intolerable burden. We should, first and foremost, be ourselves, with the job we do as one of the many masks we wear, which we are free to remove and replace with a more appropriate one whenever the need arises.

For instance, the father of a family might be a lawyer by profession and be very successful in his field of endeavour. He may go home and continue to play the same role with his wife and children, who need a husband and father, not a lawyer. At social functions, it has become a joke that if a group of doctors, lawyers or others engaged in the same or a similar occupation gather together, the conversation invariably is about their work. In other words, they are so identified with their occupational roles that the human being behind the professional role is barely visible.

The economic situation in the world, together with increased freedom for women, has resulted in many women being employed outside the home in addition to being housewives. This creates a situation where the children frequently experience having two parents who continue to wear their work masks at home. But children require the warmth and interest in their needs that is available only from real human beings, and not the cold and often mechanical reactions of two career-dominated parents. At the end of a working day the job and all its implications should be left behind at the place of work. The actual person who daily engages in the job should be available to pursue other more family-orientated activities.

Many people who work with me mention that one of their chief problems while they were growing up was that they rarely felt they knew their parents as real people. So often, the father, in particular, would be a stranger, more interested in his work than in them. He would pay the bills, but often considered that to be more than sufficient to have done for them. So they felt starved for his loving attention. Even though they knew they were loved, when there was no outward sign or expression of it, they doubted it and strove in various ways to elicit some sign of it to assuage their craving, often resorting to negative behaviour out of desperation to obtain it.

Before returning home, it would be helpful if working parents would take a few minutes to do the Figure Eight around themselves and their entire work situation. They would find that in addition to no longer bringing home the frequently heavy load of responsibilities, they would also gain a clearer perspective of their problems at work. This would enable them to deal with the problems more successfully the following day having, in the interim, ceased being so closely caught up in them.

Children can be taught from quite early on to do the same with school-work and, in the process, learn to give their entire attention to whatever they are doing at any given time. In that way a habit will have been established that will carry over into their working years in later life, and help to mitigate the frequently dehumanising effect of work.

A very different attitude to the actual work is also necessary. In the past, on the whole, people took pride in their work as a service to the community. But this attitude has changed all over the world. The current approach appears to be to do as little as possible for the most remuneration. The monetary reward now takes precedence over the workmanship, with the result that no matter what the nature of the work, there is no guarantee that it will be carried out adequately or even completed. The frustration that follows in the wake of such unreliable workers has reached epidemic proportions and adds to the already heavy load of stress most people suffer in everyday life.

If children are taught to work, not primarily for money, but for the reward of satisfaction in a job well done, and to look upon work itself as a service, a great deal of the pressure would be relieved from individuals as well as from society as a whole. It is really surprising what a great difference such a change of attitude can bring about.

Chapter 22

INHERITED AND
BEHAVIOURAL PATTERNS

To recapitulate, a newborn baby enters an already existing set of patterns. It is attracted to them because they offer it an opportunity to work out its old karma, learn the lessons it failed in other lives and, in this way, move along the inner path back to union with the High C. The two main influences are hereditary and behavioural. Those that are inherited originate from the two converging family patterns, beliefs and attitudes and everything else brought down through the generations. These include a whole host of different influences such as racial characteristics and national traits and customs. Then there are the religious affiliations, such as Jewish, Buddhist, Muslim, Hindu, Christian and others, with all their attendant mores. There are also the various social classes, seen at their most rigid in India's caste system.

The occupational background of the father (and to some extent nowadays, of the mother) also exerts its influence. Even the political affiliation, the type of area where the family lives, whether rural, town, or city and, of course, the kind of schools attended, all make their mark on the child.

In addition to all the above listed influences, there are the more personal ones projected onto the growing child by the various members of the family, mainly the parents. These may originate from the parents' own biases, expectations or fears, or develop as the child is labelled in some way by the parents, such as lazy, clever, good-looking and so forth.

There are also those influences resulting from the way the parents try to live out their own unfulfilled dreams, hopes, ambitions and desires through their children in a misguided effort to try to benefit vicariously from their children's success.

It can easily be seen that there are many patterns projected onto a child that can prevent its flourishing. Many different techniques have been forthcoming to free people from such negative conditioning. Usually, as soon as a problem is presented, a technique is provided by the High C to help to solve it. However, in a large number of cases, it is sufficient just to use the Figure Eight around the appropriate symbol for two weeks, or longer if necessary, to bring about a release from the old patterns.

Projection of Animus and Anima

We all project many parts of ourselves onto other people which are then reflected back to us. This enables us to see them more clearly. However, we invariably expect and, at times, even demand that they accept the role we have projected onto them and to bear it for us. But the role belongs to us and represents an aspect of ourselves. So it should be assumed by us and lived out through our lives when that is appropriate, not forced onto others to portray. Even though we project it onto another person, it can never fit him exactly. He has his own personality, with all its various roles. No two people are identical though they may have similar facets. But a facet is not the whole person.

By projecting parts of ourselves onto others and expecting them to assume and act them out for us, we play the role of puppeteer and try to force the other person to be a puppet dancing to our tune. But he has his own tune, which may be different from ours. At the same time, he is probably projecting some of his aspects onto us, thus creating a case of dual projection and control.

One of the most common projections is that of the anima by a man onto a likely woman as the recipient and the animus by a woman onto a likely man. The result is the development of a symbiotic relationship between the partners. In some love relationships, this could be the basis for believing that one or both the partners have found their twin soul or soul-mate. People tend to fall in love with a person who reminds them, albeit unconsciously, of the other half of themselves. They see this part as if reflected in a mirror, the other person being cast as the mirror.

We are all seeking wholeness or completion, whether or not we are aware of it. We crave union with this inner and opposite part of us. But, to become whole, we must seek it within us and avoid projecting it onto another person and expecting him or her to satisfy our need by living it out for us. Such behaviour is not only stultifying to our own growth, but places an intolerable burden on the person we have chosen to carry the particular projection. It does not belong to him, but is only partially similar and merely a part of him.

To complicate the situation even further, superimposed over our male and female parts are the personalities of our mother and/or father. When a boy starts to express his manhood and his feminine anima, and a girl her femininity and her masculine animus, each seeks role models: the first ones, naturally, are their parents. If the parents present positive role models, these will influence the child to assume them as he begins to express his own dual nature. However, the reverse is also true. If they present negative role models, he may choose to express opposite ones.

This early programming is responsible for the fact that in addition to seeking their own inner anima or animus in another person, people may also be trying to find a substitute mother or father-figure. This is especially possible if either parent has elicited a negative reaction in the growing child, by acting in an unaccepting, critical or unloving manner. Many marriages and other close relationships are actually alliances between various projected parts instead of between real people. When men seek a mother and women seek a father in their mate, they may try to force the partner to play the parent, with themselves in the roles of the children. Unfortunately, such a situation is usually very unsatisfactory in the long run. A person may, at first, be willing to assume the parental role. But, in so doing, the child within the partner remains a child and the relationship becomes static and cannot flourish. Each person needs to become a parent to his own child. No one can or should try to assume that task for another person, however close, or expect another person to take that responsibility onto himself.

We all have within us the potential to become whole and balanced individuals. But, to succeed, we need to make contact with these parts inside us and to resist the temptation to expect others to play them for us. When we have shouldered the responsibility of owning all our various facets, we can begin to allow the High C to polish them. It can then act like a diamond-cutter, cutting and polishing the facets of the diamond to bring out the brilliance hidden inside the rough outer covering.

When we have projected parts of ourselves onto others, we give these people power over us in our insistence that they assume a part of us that we ourselves ought to have accepted and demonstrated in our lives. Similarly, when we accept another person's projection, we are stealing from them their opportunity to discover it within themselves and start to use it.

None of us can become whole and balanced until we have recognised, accepted and assumed responsibility for all our own parts, both yin and yang, or feminine and masculine. These are the two poles, or sets of wiring, that can safely handle the tremendous voltage of the High C when eventually It takes over our lives.

How can we withdraw the anima or animus after we have caught sight of an aspect of it reflected in a suitable person onto whom we have projected it? First, we need to practise the Figure Eight. The person who is acting as a hat rack, or hook, on which we have hung a particular role is visualised in the circle opposite our own. The usual two weeks is generally sufficient time for this exercise to be practised. But, in more extreme cases, it may take longer.

The Tree exercise should also be practised daily. After the two Cosmic Parents have become familiar and the person feels secure – that is, accepted and loved by them, they can be asked to introduce a figure that symbolises the real and complete anima or animus. The anima should appear on the left side of a man as he is supported by the trunk of the tree. The animus should be on the right side of a woman. Initially, it is preferable not to visualise them too clearly in order to avoid the temptation to superimpose actual people on to them. Eventually, when they do surface more clearly, they may be reminiscent of one or even a combination of several known people, but they are actually individual and different from anyone else, just as a person's fingerprints are unique to him.

If either the negative or positive image of the mother or father is projected onto another person, it, too, must be withdrawn and the Cosmic Parents sought within.

None of us likes to see our own faults and weaknesses and most people will go to great lengths to avoid recognising and admitting them. It is so much easier, and less painful, to see faults in others and to criticise and judge them rather than accept and deal with our own blemishes. But it is equally wrong to project onto others the positive parts of ourselves that may have been suppressed or neglected in childhood. When this happens, we may even envy those who are expressing our repressed qualities.

One of the most frequent examples of projection that occurs in current psychological practice is that of transference of various facets of the personality onto the therapist. When the High C, with its two aspects, the Cosmic Mother and Cosmic Father, is the therapist, projection is greatly minimised. All the parts of a person can be contacted within himself as soon as he is willing to withdraw his projections from all outer people or things.

At some time, either in this life or a prior one, we have probably been like the people we now find difficult to accept; so, instead of blaming or criticising them, we need to recognise and rectify the parts of ourselves that we dislike reflected in them.

Chapter 23

SUB-PERSONALITIES

In our present state, we are not one main single personality, but a whole collection of splinters or sub-personalities within the main one, most of them unconscious. These facets are often revealed in dreams. When we dream of a person known to us we can catch sight of an aspect of ourselves represented by him or her. It is helpful to ask ourselves what those people appearing in our dreams are like. What is the first thing we think of when we pose that question? What are their most noticeable characteristics? What is our opinion of them or our attitude towards them?

We can then internalise these evaluations and accept the fact that we may be carrying within us those same characteristics, though most probably unconsciously. Having seen them in others and observed how they act in our dreams, we can begin to catch sight of them as they surface in our daily life. In this way we can start to work on eradicating those aspects that are undesirable, by placing each one in the other circle of the Figure Eight and visualising the beam of blue light flowing around it. Often, it is sufficient to do just that for two weeks. However, it is sometimes essential to recover the energy these parts of us hold locked within them, allowing them to lead their half-life inside us, their host. We can then set that energy free for our own use.

This is best accomplished by breathing the energy from the splinter part back into ourselves with each inhalation and then breathing out any further need or attachment to it with each exhalation. Then the two circles can be separated by cutting them apart, using whatever method is indicated by the High C. The circle containing the de-energised symbol can then be thrust into outer space, pushed off a precipice, dropped into the fiery crater of a volcano, or disposed of in some other way.

Another way to recognise the different facets of the personality is to watch our reactions to other people. Invariably, those whom we dislike or criticise can actually remind us of facets of ourselves of which we are unconscious, or that we do not wish to recognise. To repeat, it is so much easier to criticise someone else for a negative characteristic than to turn the searchlight onto ourselves and thus catch sight of our own faults. But the opposite is also true. We may criticise someone who is expressing a trait that for some reason we should be using, but are neglecting to do so. Again, it is easier to be critical of someone else and, by so doing, persuade ourselves that we do not need to develop that particular aspect, as it is not good anyway.

Hall of Mirrors

If these two methods fail to show us facets of our personality of which we are unconscious, another method has been given through the reverie work.

It is called the Maze, or Hall of Mirrors. It unfolded one day when I was working with a young woman who had a vague sense that she was acting in negative ways, but though she tried hard to be more specific, she failed to see the problem clearly. I suggested that she call on the High C to help her to see facets of her personality of which she was oblivious.

As soon as we had set up the triangle and had both made contact with the High C, a very clear symbol came quickly into my mind. It was a hall of mirrors like those I had seen during my childhood in amusement parks, constructed like a maze, but with all the inside walls covered with mirrors. However, they were not ordinary mirrors. Each one reflects a grossly distorted image of the person looking into it.

I explained the symbol to the young woman and asked if she would like me to lead her into the maze so that she could ask to be shown various facets of herself more clearly. She was delighted at this opportunity. So I suggested that, first, she should visualise me holding a ball of string, and herself holding the end of it to take with her as she entered the maze. She could then proceed as far as she was led by the High C and, as soon as she needed to withdraw, I would pull her back out. The string reminded her of Ariadne's thread. She said it made her feel much safer, as she was afraid of being overwhelmed by the unconscious personalities within her if she had to face too many of them at once.

The first mirror she approached reflected back a very fat image of herself. At first she rejected it, objecting that she was not overweight. I explained that it might not refer to obesity due to overeating, but to some other form of greed. She gasped in recognition, for it helped her to see a side of herself which is very greedy for recognition. She described it as always wanting to be puffed up with her own importance, ability and attractiveness.

The next mirror showed her a small yapping dog that reminded her of a terrier. Again she was at a loss to decipher the message until I told her that in this work a dog is a symbol for the extroverted part of a person, whereas a cat represents the introverted part. I then asked her which of the two she thought applied to her. She immediately replied, 'Oh, a dog, of course'. She was then able to see that the image she had been shown in the mirror was that part of her that was so greedy for attention that she acted like a yapping terrier and made a nuisance of herself by her persistent demands to be noticed.

The next mirror showed her as a forlorn child, begging for food. This image was undoubtedly the reason for the first two. She had never received from her parents or other members of her family the love and attention she craved. She had tried in numerous ways to attract their attention, but without success, so she brought with her into adulthood the same craving, still unassuaged.

At that point, she complained that she was exhausted and asked to be pulled back out, for she was sure she could not handle any further insights this time. But I received a distinct impression that she should ask to be shown if there was anything she needed to do with the three images before we ended the session. She reluctantly agreed and slowly reported that she was being shown that the forlorn little girl who had lacked love and attention needed help. When she asked the High C how to supply it, she was instructed to treat the little girl as her own inner child and give her whatever she needed with loving care. She cried quietly as she told me.

Next came the little dog. He needed to be put on a leash and trained not to make a nuisance of himself. She agreed to watch for those times when the dog-like part became overactive and too demanding, and to begin to control it.

When she came back to the first image, she startled me with a burst of anger and said she wanted to smash not only the reflection of the fat woman, but the mirror itself, to break free of the image. When I encouraged her to do so, she derived great satisfaction from hurling a large rock at the mirror and its offensive reflection. But she soon discovered that each small piece was still capable of reflecting the obnoxious figure. Her only recourse was to smash the pieces into dust with the help of a steamroller. She was still not completely satisfied until all the glass dust had been gathered up in a vacuum cleaner and deposited in a rubbish bin.

Using Clay Models to Symbolise Aspects of the Personality

Yet another method has been found to work very well in uncovering unknown facets of the personality. When a person has identified an aspect of himself that he would like to relinquish, but none of the above methods appears to be adequate, I suggest he purchase some children's modelling clay.

He then selects an activity that requires complete concentration, such as reading, listening to the radio or a cassette, or watching television, to distract his conscious mind from what he is about to do. He should then take the clay, set up a triangle and ask the High C to direct his hands to mould the clay into a symbol of that part of himself from which he wishes to be free.

Many people have followed this method with great success and the shapes they have formed, while their conscious mind was otherwise engaged have been fascinating. These models always perfectly represent the attitude or problem from which detachment is being sought.

Next, the person is instructed to visualise the Figure Eight, with the clay model in the circle opposite his own, and to practise this exercise night and morning, for the usual two-week period. At the end of that time, he can either work alone or with another person and ask the High C to show him how to transfer back into himself the energy deposited in the part of him depicted by the clay model. Some people are directed to hold the model they have fashioned, imagine it attached to them by a tube, or some other connection, and breathe in the energy. Others squeeze it between their hands to allow the energy to escape and be reabsorbed. There are countless ways to achieve freedom from domination by the part thus discovered, but it is always best to ask the High C to indicate the most appropriate method each time. The answer never fails to appear, is always suited to each individual and often comes as a complete surprise to him. Finally, the person is instructed to ask the High C how to destroy the symbol in as convincing a way as possible, to impress the subconscious that he no longer wishes that facet to be active in his life.

Chapter 24

FREEDOM FROM
FEAR OF REJECTION

One woman who came to work with me wanted to be free from a fear of rejection which was so strong that she was fully aware that she always expected to be rejected. It was almost as if she looked for it, hoping to allay the fear more quickly by getting the rejection behind her. Many people appear to share this attitude. I recall one young boy telling me that his father was extremely critical of him and would watch him, waiting for him to make a mistake. When the boy could bear the tension no longer he would deliberately make a mistake in order to satisfy his father's expectation and get it over with. The anger that always erupted from his father also broke the tension.

I suggested to the woman who feared rejection the possibility of growing to the point where she would not need to react from fear, for only then could she be free from this condition. She said she doubted that such a change would ever be possible. So I explained that the part of her that feared rejection was not her entire self, but merely one small part. When she gratefully accepted that idea, I suggested that she try to describe to me the rejected part. At first she found that task too difficult but, with further prodding, she began to engage in what she called a game. She imagined herself in a cowering posture with one arm and hand held up as if to protect herself from attack, and her body turned, ready to run at a moment's notice. As she described what she was seeing, she became aware that this attitude was literally begging for someone either to reject or attack her. She continued to verbalise her reactions to what she was observing. She said that if she could be free from that inner attitude, maybe she would also be free from the rejection she so feared and which always seemed to occur, as if she were magnetically drawing it to her.

She agreed to visualise a Figure Eight with herself in one circle and the image of her rejected self in the other for two weeks. When she returned, she reported that just seeing so clearly what she had unconsciously been doing to attract the dreaded rejection, had already freed her more than she would ever have believed possible. Now she was anxious to proceed with the cutting session, certain that it would help even more. She also realised that this fear had been growing within her since early childhood when her father deserted her and her mother. This had forced her mother to farm her out to various foster homes in order to be free to work to support them both.

I explained that her attitude of expecting, or of almost demanding, rejection originated first in the rejection by her father and then again by her mother when she was too young to understand the reasons for it. I reminded her that this attitude was only a part of herself and not the whole. She was able to understand this even more clearly after the two-week period of visualising the Figure Eight had given her a different perspective and a partial sense of freedom.

When she arrived for the cutting session, we set up the Triangle and the Figure Eight and I suggested that she ask the High C what she should do with her symbolic picture of rejection. The answer she received came as a surprise to her. She was told to love it. At first, she rebelled and said that not only could she not love it, but that she hated it for causing her so much suffering. I told her to forget for a moment that it was a part of herself and think of it as a frightened little girl needing her help. If that were actually the case, what would she do? Immediately, she replied that she would talk to her and ask her how she could help. She proceeded to do so and reported that the girl told her that she felt she must have done something terrible to cause her father to leave. Then, when her mother left her with strangers, she decided she must be very bad indeed and thoroughly deserving of the harsh treatment being meted out to her; yet, at the same time, she was always afraid of what might happen next.

I suggested she take the little girl to the Tree and introduce her to the Cosmic Parents. She was delighted and said it took some of the mounting sense of heavy responsibility off her shoulders. She continued to care for her inner rejected child with the help of her Cosmic Parents and gradually lost her former incapacitating fear of rejection. As she became free of its control, she realised that she no longer experienced rejection, simply because she no longer attracted it to her by fearing it.

Some people are shown a negative part of themselves in a dream. It can be personified by a person known to the dreamer or a character in the dream acting in a certain way that is reminiscent of the way he himself sometimes acts.

The procedure for eliminating this negative facet is the same as that outlined above. The person first visualises the Figure Eight around himself and the symbol he has seen in his dream for the usual two weeks. During that time, he may have many unexpected insights which will clarify the condition.

Chapter 25

TRADITIONS, CUSTOMS AND MORES

We are all destined to our share of the heritage of the family we were born into. That includes the racial and national customs of both parents. Originally, customs and taboos were developed for specific purposes, such as a health safeguard to prevent contamination from other groups, or to act as guidelines to daily life.

Gradually, the original meaning of the customs was lost and they persisted only as traditional do's, don'ts and traditions. But without the awareness of the original meaning they became empty and rigid and, in some instances, their importance was so distorted that they became actively harmful.

The degeneration of customs can be detected all over the world in the various cultural groups. This is particularly noticeable in the major religions where the rituals have lost their original meaning and have become empty exercises lacking the inspiration capable of raising people's consciousness, which was their original intent. Our true heritage, based as it is on truth, is precious. It is the overlay of falsity accumulated over the centuries, and which is hiding it from sight, that needs to be removed.

Many old customs which had meaning for the people at the time of their formation by leaders and other wise ones, are no longer appropriate in a world which has changed so much so quickly.

It is not necessary to cut the ties to any customs or beliefs that still have meaning and are useful to the society in which they were formulated. These still have the ability to help those who subscribe to them to progress towards oneness with the High C, whereas the rigid and constricting ones can obstruct the inner journey. Appropriate symbols of some of these old useless patterns are needed to help people to free themselves from their influence so that they can move ahead towards wholeness.

We must learn how to let go of the past. It is gone for ever and can never return however much we wish we could retrieve it. Neither can we do anything now to change it. It is therefore useless to live in the past with old memories. We can put a symbol of anything from the past that still controls us and cut the ties that bind us to it. Likewise, we should not try to live in the future for it is also beyond our direct control. That, too, is a waste of valuable time and energy. It is best to live as effectively as possible in the present, learning the lessons we may have failed to learn in the past. By living in the 'now' honestly and conscientiously, we are determining our future. Our actions of the past are affecting us now, and those we initiate now will bear fruit in the future. This is a law that cannot be flouted. The truth of the old proverb, 'As ye sow, so shall ye reap,' may not be immediately discernible but when the time and conditions are right, either in this life or at some future time, it will become apparent.

One very important point we should always bear in mind is that nothing and no one in the outer world is permanent, so nothing can or should be considered an eternal possession. This also applies to traditions, customs and mores that are currently of little or no value.

Chapter 26

PREJUDICES

Other thought-patterns imprinted upon us during childhood, primarily by the parents, are the erroneous blanket attitudes towards national groups other than our own.

Prejudices go hand in hand with chauvinism. The most extreme example of this national superiority was observed during the Nazi regime in Germany. Hitler's belief in Aryan supremacy was accepted by his followers with the attendant degradation and eventual extermination of countless numbers of Jews in an effort to prevent them from contaminating the 'superior' race.

If we take seriously the concept that a spark of divinity or life is carried within everything and everyone in the whole of creation and that all the sparks are identical, then it makes no sense at all to elevate one group or person above all others, or to discriminate against other groups or individuals as being worthless or despicable.

All peoples need to be re-educated to accept humanity as a whole. Snobbery can work both ways. Some people consider themselves superior to others, while some have the opposite attitude and think they are inferior. The latter is an inverted snobbery and is just as narrow and restrictive as its opposite.

Throughout history, certain groups of people, such as the English, Germans and Chinese, have espoused the concept of superiority to a greater extent than others. But the Jews, despite the fact that they have always been taught that they were God's chosen people and therefore superior, have been debased and harassed and made the scapegoat by other national groups, causing great suffering. It is to be hoped that a balanced and more realistic opinion of their worth will eventually emerge, as more people cut the ties to old attitudes.

National Characteristics

National characteristics are frequently at the root of such prejudice. We have each been born in a particular country which used to determine our nationality. However, in recent times, since travel has become so much easier, such is not always the case. Most of the racial groups lived in distinct and separate countries or areas, but this too is no longer always true. As an example, in the United States, there are many racial groups all living side by side in the same town or city. The beginning of a movement appears to be taking place in the world that will eventually break down the barriers between separate groups. Hopefully, this will lead to a world family in place of many racial or religious groups often fighting one another for supremacy. Intermarriage between individuals from different races and cultures is hastening this process.

I distinctly remember as a child growing up in England being told over and over again that I must never forget how fortunate I was to be born English. In my innocence, I once asked why this was so. It seemed to me that I could just as easily have been born French, Italian or Japanese. I remember to this day the way my mother reacted with such horror and anger that I never repeated the question for fear of more dire consequences. I was taught that all other nations were inferior to the English, and that some were even more inferior than others. Unfortunately, this kind of smugness has become attached like a label to the English and badly needs to be discarded.

Why, I used to wonder, was I born in England of English heritage in that particular family, to those two parents, with the conditioning from all the factors attendant upon that birth? As I look back now from the vantage-point of all that I have been taught by the High C, I realise that my entire background has given me the opportunities to experience those very things I needed in order to learn certain lessons. I doubt they could have been learned as thoroughly in a different culture or family. However, I did not know that while I was growing up. I was, like any other young child, living on an unconscious and mostly automatic level of action and reaction to outer stimuli. But, since I have been receiving the inner instruction and have retrieved what I was led to believe were past lives, I can see that I have been given the opportunities, frustrations, difficulties and problems most likely to push me along the inner path. They have also forced me to search for meaning, not just to this life, but to the long history of many lifetimes, all leading to the eventual goal of liberation or enlightenment, when the ego finally merges with the High C.

Other nations have had different labels attached to them, such as miserly, arrogant, frivolous, devious, melancholy, conscientious, avaricious, hot-tempered, calculating, emotional, impractical, materialistic, untrustworthy, lazy, impulsive, impetuous and many others. If these national traits are used as a challenge by individuals born into each of the different cultures, they can enable them to learn those things for which they entered the world in that particular milieu.

No one is obliged to identify with the negative traits. All are free to cultivate the positive attributes of their country. In the same way that all are free to detach themselves from negative aspects of the personality, it is equally possible and certainly advisable to cut oneself off from them at the national level as well.

Our identity is not governed by our nationality any more than our worth is dictated by how much money we have, nor how brilliant, famous, attractive, sophisticated or well-dressed we are in the eyes of the world.

Individual Attachments

In addition to the foregoing general attachments or controlling customs, it is very helpful to start making a list of specifically personal ones and continue to add to it whenever others are observed during the course of the day.

It is not a matter of doing without the people, places, things or ideas to which we are attached, but rather of holding on to them lightly instead of tightly, as if they were merely borrowed for a limited length of time. This attitude makes it easier to relinquish them when the need arises or at the time of death.

It is advisable to use the Figure Eight around anything that it would be hard to do without. Just practising it gives perspective and helps to show that the object or person is not indispensable or permanent, but separate from its temporary owner, with its own destiny to fulfil. This exercise brings about a much more flowing relationship with people and far less fear of the loss of loved ones or favourite possessions.

Chapter 27

WORLD RELIGIONS
AND THEIR EFFECTS

Assuming a belief in reincarnation, it seems probable that we have incarnated into many ethnic groups besides our present one and have, therefore, been exposed to various religious beliefs other than those of our present family.

The basic tenets of all established religions are very similar. Each one teaches that love is a guiding force in the world and that it should be extended to others beyond the narrow circle of the immediate family. Another tenet common to all religions is that we should treat others as we would wish them to treat us.

In very early times, God, or the source of all life, was thought to be a female, a Mother-Goddess. It is believed that the reason for this concept arose when primitive people observed that new life in the form of a baby issued from a woman and never from a man. Man's role in the formation of a new being was probably not understood. It was therefore assumed that the Creator or Originator of the world must be feminine. Some of the earliest sculptures are of mother/fertility goddesses.

Gradually, the understanding of the man's role dawned on some groups and the belief developed that the male role was the more important. Without impregnation by a man a woman could not bear children, so people began to project on to God, the Great

Creator, a masculine image. This belief has continued in many parts of the world to this day. It is only slowly beginning to be replaced in more forward-thinking groups and individuals by the concept of a combined Mother-Father God. Actually, in India, the dual concept has been accepted for centuries. The clearest representation of it being Shiva-Shakti, where the assertive or active part of God is presented as Shiva and the feminine energy as Shakti.

In the West with the advent of psychology, and particularly with Carl Jung's contributions to this field, the dual role within everyone is being accepted and understood by more and more people. The terms *anima* and *animus*, introduced by Carl Jung, have made it much easier to accept and discuss the dual role which is everyone's birthright.

The Chinese have always referred to these two different energies as *yin* for feminine and *yang* for masculine. Their symbol representing the combination of the two acting together in all living things is a circle divided by a wavy line into two parts, in which a dark spot, or *yin*, is placed in the light, or *yang*, side and a light spot, or *yang*, in the dark, or *yin*, side. The dark signifies the feminine and the light the masculine energies, but each contains a part of the other. Apparently, the wise men in each main race of people received inspirationally or intuitively the original form of their belief and method of worship, which was designed to guide them in their daily life in the most practical manner. Each set of rules and customs was valid for a particular race or group. They were all slightly different from one another, but none can in any sense be thought better than others.

Over long periods of time, these original tenets gathered layers of beliefs and practices laid down by priests and/or shamans. They had their own reasons, a principal one being to gain control over the people. In this way, the differences between the world religions became more marked. But, unfortunately, the differences rather than the similarities of the original forms were emphasised, followers of each system averring that theirs was the only correct path to God. But all paths lead eventually to union with God. No one path is any better or more direct than any other, merely better suited to the temperament of a particular culture.

The pure core of teaching in each belief system should be retained. But it is necessary to detach oneself from erroneous practices, rules, teachings, superstitions, fears and taboos that have grown up around that central core, since it is these that bind people and render them incapable of pursuing their path back to the Godhead.

Some examples may help to illustrate methods that have successfully removed from individuals the outer trappings of some of the belief systems. They can then be applied according to individual situations.

Christianity

I will start with the effect of the Christian religion, since it was the one espoused by my parents and therefore more familiar to me. Jesus's words and deeds, as reported in the New Testament in a few very brief accounts, were recorded quite some time after his death. Consequently, they are sparse and quite probably even erroneous in parts, since man's memory is not always reliable. But even this meagre documentary of his life and message reveals a simple yet very practical teaching which he himself acted out in his daily life. Because it was so basic, it still retains meaning for us today.

However, so much doctrine has grown up around the original simple teaching that the true message Jesus sought to give to the world has been almost lost beneath the overwhelming structure erected by the Church. Many times in the past, reformers have arisen and tried to pare away some of the encrustations of unnecessary dogma. But each time a new structure developed, it gradually lost sight of the true spirit of the message Jesus came to deliver.

Many of the sects of Christianity share the common belief that Jesus assumes responsibility for believers' sins, thus removing all responsibility from the individual. In addition, pardon by a cleric, as in the Catholic practice of confession, leaves a person free to repeat his failings instead of working to overcome them to allow him to become a mature and disciplined individual.

Two conflicting messages are often taught; one that Jesus took upon himself the sins of his followers, while the other teaches that sinners will be damned and go the hell. Some of the lurid descriptions of what they are likely to suffer in hell are often described in terrifying terms. But these teachings are man-made and designed to give the Church control over the congregations instead of allowing them to develop their own ability to make direct contact with the High C. The so-called heretics who sought to be guided from within rather than by the organised Church were not merely ostracised but frequently tortured, put to death or imprisoned. The Spanish Inquisition is an example of this kind of power over parishioners. Such domination is saddening and far from the teachings of Jesus which emphasised love for one another. Unfortunately, however, when the founder of a religion or sect is no longer alive the organisation built up around his mission often becomes rigid and stultified, and no longer allows individuals to experience the living message.

Of all the many sects of Christianity, the Roman Catholic Church has, perhaps, the most lasting control over its adherents. Jesuits – members of a Catholic sect renowned for teaching – are wont to declare that if they have control of a child until the age of 7, he will be faithful to the teachings for the rest of his life. This can be likened to living under the control, not merely of two parents, but of a whole army of disciplinary figures.

One reason why the effect of Catholicism on a young child is so much stronger than other Christian sects is probably because the rituals include inspirational music, incense, the rich and colourful vestments of the clergy, and the Latin in which some of the prayers and hymns are intoned, all appealing strongly to the senses and therefore penetrating directly to the subconscious with very little censoring or conscious processing.

Perhaps, one of the most common results of this early discipline is the deep-seated guilt and fear which are often carried throughout an entire lifetime. The usual techniques for removing such negative conditions, such as the Jack for fear and the Wet Suit for guilt (see *Cutting the Ties that Bind* for details), are not completely effective when their root cause lies in the early exposure to the Roman Catholic version of Christianity, simply because its influence is so strong and lasting.

Some people who have been raised as Catholics say they feel as if they were bound hand and foot by the 'Thou shalts and thou shalt nots'. Many long to be free. Some do rebel and break the ties, to all intents and purposes, but they eventually discover that they are still firmly bound at a very deep level of their being, however much they try to break free.

After several encounters with both men and women who felt so constricted, I was shown how to help them free themselves from the imprisoning effects of their Catholic upbringing. One woman knew immediately the symbol that for her represented the constriction she felt. She recalled herself as a child staring up at the huge cold marble-like statue portraying the Virgin Mary in the church where she sat with her family every Sunday. She used to try to imagine that figure being loving and comforting. But the more she tried, the colder it appeared. Her own parents were very cold and critical so, as a little girl, she had instinctively turned to Mother Mary for the love she so craved. But again she was disappointed.

I suggested that she put this cold statue in the other circle of the Figure Eight and practise the exercise for the prescribed two-week period. As she began this exercise, she reported that unexpected surges of anger began welling up within her. She felt cheated at having been taught that Jesus came to teach love when she lacked any sign of it in her life.

At the end of the two weeks, she was eager to cut herself free from the cold and forbidding symbol. As soon as she was sufficiently relaxed, she asked the High C to indicate what should be done to release her from bondage. She was aghast at the answer she received and cried so hysterically that she could not tell me what it was for several minutes. When at last she regained some semblance of composure, she haltingly reported that she was being directed to take a sledge-hammer and smash the statue to pieces. It took a long time to convince her that this would not be the sacrilege she feared, since the cold statue was merely a symbol and not the actual mother of Jesus.

Finally, she was willing to try to follow the directions she had been given. As soon as she acquiesced, she described being handed a hammer in her inner scene. With it she proceeded to attack the statue with such venom that my heart ached for the little girl who grew up with that cold image of motherhood. As she proceeded with the demolition, she gained courage and began to enjoy the release of her pent-up frustrations.

Suddenly, she stopped describing what was happening and, finally, gasped out in an awestruck whisper, 'Oh, the most beautiful angelic figure has emerged from the broken statue and is standing smiling at me.' She described how her surprise visitor was dressed in a sky-blue robe with the most wonderful light streaming out from all over her. With tears pouring down her cheeks, she hesitantly told me, 'She is beckoning to me to go to her. Should I go?' When I gently asked if she would like to, without any further hesitation and with heartfelt intensity, she said, 'Oh yes.'

I remained quiet for some time while she was intent on watching her inner scene, with tears continuing to stream unheeded from her eyes. Later she was able to tell me that she had flung herself into the outstretched arms of the luminous figure. She could actually feel herself being held tightly as she snuggled against the soft, comforting body of this real mother whom she had sought so desperately, though unsuccessfully, all her life.

Before she emerged from this inner experience, I suggested that she ask to be shown what to do with the broken pieces of stone that had so completely covered the warm, loving presence she had discovered hidden beneath it. She was silent for a few minutes, then told me that they had been ground to dust by a huge steamroller. Quite casually she remarked that they would form a nice smooth surface for her inner path.

I next suggested that she accompany her newly found mother to her tree, where she could personify the Cosmic Mother, the feminine aspect of the High C. From that time on, the figure represented for her the Cosmic Mother whenever she used the Tree exercise. Before this episode, she had not been able to see or feel a Cosmic Mother figure at all and was only barely aware of the Cosmic Father.

A Catholic man with whom I worked was so guilt-ridden that he was afraid to do anything lest it be a mortal sin. He leaped at the chance to gain release from effects of a particular childhood memory: the punitive behaviour of one of his schoolteachers.

He, too, knew immediately the symbol he would use for the Catholic Church as he had experienced it. He described a Crucifix which had hung above the altar in the church he and his family used to attend. It was a life-size figure of Christ nailed to the Cross with realistic looking blood gushing from the many wounds around his head, where the thorns of the mock crown had pierced the flesh, from the large gash in his side made by the spear that had been thrust into it, and from his hands and feet where the nails had pierced them.

This figure was so frightening to the little boy that it became a symbol of the kind of punishment that would be meted out to him if he committed a sin. Consequently, he was terrified to do anything that could possibly be considered wrong, for fear of such dire retribution. This terrible fear had haunted him unabated during his entire childhood and into adulthood. So he was eager to start visualising the Figure Eight around himself, with the awesome suffering figure in the opposite circle. He told me that just knowing that freedom from this childhood nightmare was possible made him feel freer than he had felt in years.

At the end of two weeks he returned, excited at the prospect of being set free. As soon as he was relaxed, he asked the High C how he should proceed and was instantly silent. I wondered if he might have fallen asleep, as sometimes happens if the emotions are too overpowering. After a suitable interval, I very gently asked what was happening. In a scared little voice he said, 'I was shown that I must be willing to wash his wounds.' He was obviously appalled at the idea and balked at continuing with the reverie. I told him it was only a statue, but it had apparently been so very real to him as a child that he was terrified of the task he had been given.

I asked if he would like me to help him. After another long pause, while he considered this proposal, he shook his head, saying he knew he must have the courage to do it himself. So I directed him to ask the High C to send down his side of the triangle we had erected between us the necessary courage to do whatever was needed to free him from the overwhelming terror that had paralysed him for so long.

He started to breathe deeply as he inhaled the energy which he said he could actually feel flowing into him from the High C. After about a dozen deep breaths, he said he was ready to start, so I suggested he ask the High C for help and he gratefully complied. He next reported that he had been handed a large bowl of warm water and a sponge. A ladder had also appeared in front of him, leading up to the statue of the hanging figure.

His breathing became very heavy as he worked on his inner scene. After a while he reported that he had almost removed the bloodstains from all the wounds. Suddenly, his body literally jumped as he exclaimed aloud in utter disbelief that the figure of Jesus had suddenly come to life and was coming down from the Cross, just as if he were still alive. But, he informed me in an awestruck voice, the living one looked very different from the one portrayed on the Cross. He went on to describe a vibrant, strong, very large, masculine figure with the most wonderfully deep penetrating eyes from which he could feel such love pouring out to him as he had never before experienced.

There ensued a deeply moving interaction between him and Jesus which he did not verbalise. It was obviously for him alone. At one point during the inner meeting, tears started to flow and soon he was sobbing as if he were still a child, pouring out his sadness, loneliness and feelings of overwhelming guilt to his new confidante.

Gone were the crippling fears and guilt from that time on. However, he did have fleeting flashes of the old patterns from time to time, which I assured him was only natural. These habits had slowly developed over many years so they would take time to be completely dispersed. I suggested he watch his thoughts and behaviour. Whenever he caught sight of the old attitude operating, he could shrug his shoulders and remind himself that he had no further need of it, and then release it.

The Protestant Church

The effect of the Protestant Church does not have such a profound impact in childhood. However, children are often left with their questions either unanswered, not taken seriously or answered inadequately.

Since my parents were active members of the Church of England, a Protestant Church, I will share my own experience of cutting from that belief system.

As a little girl growing up in England, I must have brought with me into this life some very definite ideas of my own. From a very early age I questioned the way that church-goers were kind and loving on Sundays, but often the exact opposite the rest of the week. Perhaps the most frustrating part, however, was not having my questions answered or my doubts allayed. I resented the lack of freedom to ask questions to satisfy my natural curiosity. I also rebelled at being told that I was special because I was a Christian.

As I look back, I distinctly remember being very angry every Sunday at the enforced attendance at church, frequently as many as three times a day. In those days there was no public transportation on Sundays, the day of rest, and it was long before cars were owned by many English families. So, we were obliged to walk several miles to the church and back to attend the services. This, together with kneeling for long hours contributed to a most embarrassing experience of regularly fainting during the service.

The result of such frustration was that as soon as I left home and came to the United States, I began a search for more meaning to life. This quest took me into some orthodox doctrines, but also some very unorthodox ones. The list is lengthy and includes the various Buddhist practices, Sufism, Vedanta, Kahuna, various types of Yoga, T'ai Chi, Transcendental Meditation, some of the strange sects I discovered in California, and many more. From each one I gleaned a valuable grain of wisdom but none completely satisfied my craving for more direct contact with what I began to call the Source.

Eventually, the reverie work gave me access to my own inner truth and when I met Sathya Sai Baba many years later, I found his teachings to be identical to all I had been taught from the High C. Baba teaches that all paths up the mountain lead to union with the Divine, and that none should be criticised or discredited referring, of course, to the pure truth each contains and not the overlay of man-made doctrine.

I work with people from many different religious backgrounds and invariably, the originator of each belief system will appear at the apex of the Triangle to represent the High C. When a Christian comes for help a figure of the Christos, the Spirit animating Jesus, often appears. I am always awed at the tremendous energy and power, together with the love that he emanates; so different from the sometimes insipid paintings we are accustomed to connect with him.

So, when I began to make contact with his Spirit in this way I realised that I had rebelled, not at this concept of Christ, but at the way his teachings had been presented to me as a child. I knew that I must cut the ties to the old view I had been taught so that I could espouse the unadulterated form of his message.

Yet, what symbol should I place in the circle opposite my own in the Figure Eight in preparation for the cutting, not from Jesus himself, but from the way he and his teachings had been presented to me as a child?

As I asked to be shown by the High C a symbol that would effectively represent this for me, I was taken back in memory to my childhood and felt I was once again sitting with my parents in a pew in the country church we had attended looking up at the minister who was preaching the Sunday sermon from the very high pulpit way above my head. Since I had consciously understood very little of what he was saying, I used to watch his gestures and facial expressions, hoping for some evidence that his message was reassuring me that I was loved and not a miserable sinner. I usually developed a stiff neck from bending my head back far enough for me to see him perched up so high above me. He and the church in which I sat seemed to create a barrier between me and what I most wanted: understanding, love and acceptance, since I was given none of these by my mother.

After the two week practice period with the Figure Eight, I was ready to sever any ties to this symbol of frustration from my childhood. To my immense surprise, I could find no ties to the figure on the pulpit, so I asked the High C to show me what I must do to free myself from this old obstacle to the Spirit of Christianity which I knew lay behind it.

I was immediately transferred from the church to my Tree and the Cosmic Parents. From that secure place I was able to visualise cutting apart the two circles of the Figure Eight and pushing the Christian symbol off into space. Immediately, the powerful Christos figure I had seen so many times when I worked with Christians appeared before me. I had been allowed to make contact with this figure in my work and now, when I was finally ready, it was very easy to accept his real message to replace the old one.

Judaism

Another man, born into a Jewish family, had a similar problem to that of the Catholic man, though it originated from a very different background. He suffered from the haunting concept of an angry and punishing God. Yet, at the same time, he had been taught that because he was Jewish, he was one of God's chosen people and must therefore live and act up to that standard. This dual programming produced an inner conflict. On the one hand he was bowed down beneath a feeling of unworthiness and inadequacy because he could never live up to what he had been taught were God's stringent expectations from His people, which appeared to him to be totally impossible to achieve; on the other hand, he realised that he must be special since he belonged to a group of people whom God had chosen. The inner confusion produced by this early programming was still rendering him ineffective and incapable of attaining success in any venture he undertook, and yet, at the same time, he was driven to succeed.

I suggested that he ask to be shown a symbol to represent his problem. One came immediately into his mind. It was the Talmud, containing the basic writings of Judaism. It includes all the laws plus the commentaries of the elders, laid down over the centuries, together with endless examples of their application, which hid from sight the few original laws given to the people to help them in their daily lives.

After the usual two-week period of visualising the Figure Eight around himself and the Talmud, he was ready for the cutting session. The actual form his symbol took was a huge black iron repository, or safe, containing all the variations on the teachings. He strongly felt they were no longer helpful to him, or practical, or relevant to his life at this time in history. Yet they still held power over him because of the control they continued to wield over his parents, who had inherited them from their families in turn.

When faced with the need to find a way to dispose of the box and all it signified to him, he was at a complete loss. He said he felt he had been carrying it around with him throughout his life. I suggested he ask the High C for help. In an incredulous voice, he told me what he needed to do. He had to separate the two circles forming the Figure Eight and push the one containing the offensive black iron box over the edge of an active volcano and into the crater, where it would completely disintegrate in the white hot lava in its depths.

The relief he expressed after he had put this suggestion into practice, literally, freed his physical body from its habitual tension, right before my eyes, as he sat in the chair in my room.

We then discussed the value of his heritage and he began to understand that despite the overwhelming burden he had carried, he had learned a great deal from it. He was now able to see that stripped of the accretions that had grown up around the original teachings was a body of knowledge that was as applicable today as when it was first received. With this wisdom he thought he could live and, eventually, he could even teach it to his children, should he have any.

Christian Science

Many Jews who convert to Christianity choose to join a Christian Science church, this apparently being a simpler step than joining any of the other Christian sects. One woman who came to work with me had been born into a Jewish family, but the parents espoused Christian Science when she was in her early teens. The effect of this on the family created many problems. This girl and her other siblings rebelled at the abrupt change from the way of life and beliefs to which they were accustomed. The confusion regarding their identity was also a problem, as was the need to explain the conversion to their friends. They felt they did not really belong, either with their Jewish friends and acquaintances or with the new Christian Science group with which they were being encouraged to mix.

So great was the woman's anger at not really knowing where she belonged that I suggested she work first on freeing herself from this old problem. I asked her what symbol would contain for her the essence of the negative reaction to be used with the Figure Eight exercise.

She chose a photograph of her mother sitting in her rocking chair with a book in her hand, reading studiously. When I asked the title of the book, she replied sarcastically, 'Mary Baker Eddy's *Keys to the Scriptures*. What else would she be reading?'

At the end of the two-week period, she returned to do the cutting. Imagine her surprise when she observed that the book her mother was holding started to get bigger and bigger until it was so large that it completely hid her from sight. Simultaneously, she felt two rods of iron begin to grow out from the front of her own forehead, apparently to push away the vision of her mother so completely identified with the book. She received directions from the High C to cut the two circles apart with an axe and push away into outer space the one containing her image of her mother and the book. The iron bars needed to be pushed back into her own head since she had projected them out with mental energy in a desperate effort to repel the hated problem. Shortly after this session, she reported that her anger had also left her.

Mormonism

One man who worked with me belonged to a family who had been Mormons for several generations. He was intelligent, had a quick mind and rebelled against what he felt were excessively rigid practices. He had already made the decision to seek expulsion from the church, to the horror of his entire family every one of whom were Mormons. So strongly did he feel about his decision, that he had repeatedly sent in a request to the Elders to consider his case. He received no reply for over a year and concluded that they wished to ignore it. He continued to write at regular intervals and was finally given a date to appear before the committee, to be questioned about his decision.

Just before receiving the date, he heard about this work and came to see me. He wanted to know if I would be willing to help him to cut the ties to the Mormon Church on the inner plane as he was about to do on the outer one. When asked to find a symbol of what he wished to cut out of his life, he visualised a group of black-robed Elders frowning in disapproval.

We were obliged to postpone the cutting appointment and, oddly enough, it was finally set for the morning of the day on which he was due, later, to appear before the Elders. He had told me he had decided to refuse to give his reasons for his decision to break with the Church, as he did not wish to undergo the interrogation he had heard would take place when they tried to convince him of his mistake.

The cutting session was brief and to the point. He was so certain of his need to break these old ties and be free to worship in his own way that he was keen to accomplish it as fast as possible. With extraordinary precision he proceeded to cut through a thick rope he reported he could see and feel around his neck like a noose or vice. Whenever he tried to pull away, it became tighter and threatened to throttle him. It had so badly chafed his neck that healing was needed. I explained that he could ask the High C to send the required healing energy down his side of the triangle we had set up between us at the start of the session. As soon as he reported that he could feel it as a tingling sensation in his body, I suggested that he place his two hands around his neck and direct the energy he was receiving into the sore area.

He then told me that he had always had difficulty in speaking and often, as a child, would gag as though about to choke, for no apparent reason. I had noticed that he rarely spoke above a whisper, so I suggested that he might like to shout as loudly as he could. At first he was reluctant to do so. After a few unsuccessful attempts, he let out a roar and was himself surprised to hear the powerful sound of his own voice when it finally broke forth. He called the next day to tell me that the interview went quite smoothly and he was now free to worship as he chose.

Communism

A man who had been working with me for only a short time decided to tell me something he had always tried to hide. He recounted his story of growing up in a family who were card-bearing Communists. This case may not appear on the surface to fit this section, as Communism is not exactly a formal religion, quite the reverse. But it had affected him as a rigid doctrine in his childhood.

His father was well known in the small community where they lived, so the family's affiliation was no secret. It made him appear different from all the other children at school. His family did not attend any church, or the social gatherings usually connected to a church or temple. He was not allowed to remain in the classroom during religious instruction which was, at that time, part of the school curriculum. He was ostracised and referred to as a Commie by his peers.

'The hammer and sickle' was his immediate response when I asked what symbol for Communism he would choose to visualise in the circle opposite his own in the Figure Eight. After the usual two-week practice, he returned to cut himself free from this hated symbol out of his unhappy childhood. As soon as he was relaxed, I asked what the High C was indicating he should do. He said he saw the hammer and sickle like a huge label he had been forced to wear, proclaiming that he belonged to a belief system which the rest of his world feared and despised.

As he watched the inner scene, he reported that the label grew bigger and bigger until it seemed to cover him so completely that he was no longer visible beneath it. He realised with a shock that he had lost his own identity. He was visibly upset to discover the extent to which he had been affected.

I suggested that he ask to be shown how to remove and destroy this badge which had caused him so much pain and embarrassment as a child. He was very quiet for several minutes and, finally, said in a small voice. 'It completely covers me. I cannot possibly remove it myself. It is bigger than I am and much stronger. I feel paralysed beneath it.'

I asked his permission to help, which he willingly gave, and I entered the inner scene with him. What I saw was a strange sight. He was in one circle of the Figure Eight. In the other circle was a tiny boy completely covered over with what looked like a huge flag on which was appliquéd the hammer and sickle.

I knew from this picture that a part of him had been suppressed at an early age. Hidden beneath the symbol, it had not been free to move on with the rest of his growing body and personality. He heartily agreed and begged me to help free him from the old stigma so that the undeveloped part could begin to catch up with the rest of him.

When I asked to be shown how to help him, I saw that I would need to cut the flag or badge away from him as if it were a second skin. With the aid of a razor blade, I proceeded to remove it from all over his body. I was not surprised to discover that it was tangled around his penis, threatening to strangle it. He told me later that he had always suffered from impotence on every level, including the sexual.

The constricting covering took a long time to remove. When asked how he would destroy it, he decided to burn it in a red hot furnace until it was reduced to ashes and no longer capable of incapacitating him. The small boy who had been buried beneath it needed to be accepted by the grown man in whom he had been hidden. I told him to imagine taking this inner child with him wherever he went and whatever he was doing. He needed to talk to him, accept him, reassure him, teach him, console and encourage him until this part grew to be his present age. It would then become a useful part of his personality instead of a hurt, embarrassed and childish part, constantly reminding him of his unhappy childhood by erupting from the subconscious at the most inconvenient moments.

Chapter 28

REINCARNATION AND KARMA

I have been taught that, during our many lives, we have lived principally under the control of the ego. Our thoughts, words and deeds have been motivated by our ego to satisfy its desires and its need to control our lives. The ego dominated our consciousness and thus prevented the High C from taking charge.

These ego-initiated thoughts, words and deeds from all the various personalities we have assumed in our many existences in the world are thought-forms filled with our energy. Energy is used to think, speak and act. But energy is neutral, neither good nor bad, positive nor negative. It is the thought-form, or body in which it is clothed, or which contains it, that determines whether the thought, word or deed will have a positive or negative effect. So, we part with some of our energy every time we think, speak or act. But our energy, in whatever form it is confined, always makes its way back to us like a homing pigeon. Sometimes it returns immediately but, more often, lifetimes later, whenever the circumstances in our lives are conducive to its return. The thought-forms containing it are rather like boomerangs thrown with a certain amount of force that determines how far they will go, or when they will hit their mark. They return to their senders with a force commensurate to the energy used in launching them.

So if, in the past, we have used our energy to harm another person by thought, word or deed, the actual thought-form containing the energy will return to us in an equally negative form. This is very different from the commonly held theory, that it is usually someone outside ourselves who hurts us. Yes, others are used to facilitate the return of our past acts, but we could not receive them unless we ourselves had first set them in motion.

The same is true of positive thoughts, words and deeds. These also return to us at some time when the circumstances allow us to reabsorb them. Since thought precedes words and deeds, it is thought that gives them form, which is the reason we call thoughts that result in words and actions thought-forms. We are their originators or creators, but we are also the recipients of all our past words and actions.

If, however, we ask the High C to think, speak and act through us each day, all day, It will initiate our thoughts, words and deeds. Then the personal self will not be responsible and need not receive the reactions, good or bad. We will be free to remain detached from the fruit of our actions, since they were not initiated by the ego. We can then be in the world without being immersed in it. This means that we cannot claim any credit for the successes or blame for the failures. That is the way to detachment. So, in each new life, we need to ask ourselves repeatedly, 'Will this act, thought or word take me nearer to the goal or further away from it?' The answer should dictate our behaviour.

We are drawn back each time into incarnation by our attachment to tangible things, people and places, as well as the intangible desires for power, position, success, and so on. Our task is clear. We need to find out who or what has the power to control us and is preventing us from freely expressing our own true selves; and who or what is preventing us from saying, with full conviction, 'Thy will, not mine, be done.' But it is not enough merely to say it. We have to live that decision on a day-to-day basis. Our lives can then become instruments for the God within us to use to bring about Its plan, not just for ourselves, but for the whole world.

With this theory in mind, we need to accept whatever occurs in our lives. But we should also understand that they are not directed at us by a cruel fate; they are the result of our own behaviour some time in the past.

But we need not allow these returning missiles to render us helpless or depressed. There is a great deal we can learn from them. We should ask ourselves repeatedly, 'What has this to teach me? How can I benefit from it?' We certainly should not sink helplessly beneath the weight of what we label problems, but which are actually opportunities.

The ancient writings of many cultures teach that we re-enter the world in a human body in circumstances suited to our past deeds and what it is that we still need to learn. This is the theory of *karma*. We all have free will and are free to learn from our self-chosen new circumstances and move along the evolutionary path. Or, we can waste the opportunity by either resisting and refusing to learn, or choosing to indulge our desires. And that automatically attaches us still more firmly to the unreal and transitory world instead of making it easier for us to be free from its influence.

Each time we take a new birth, we enter the world arena at a different stage in the evolution of human civilisation as a whole in addition to our individual one. We may be born in a male or a female body, in one or other of the many racial groups or countries with their varying cultures. Sometimes, birth into a wealthy family can offer the best opportunity for growth; at other times, being born into a poor family can provide a setting more conducive to learning. There are countless possibilities. The pure spirit is not any of these personalities, but we need to learn the lessons they provide and wring from them all the learning they offer.

I have also been taught that groups of souls can incarnate together, though not all the members are necessarily embodied at the same time. The hackneyed concept of the 'soul-mate' or 'twin soul' is not to be inferred from this statement. Each of us is born an individual in order to learn certain lessons. No one can achieve that for another. These soul groups are not only composed of people in our life who are loving and kind, but also those who cause us the most problems. The latter can spur us on to further advancement by making us so miserable that we are finally forced to bestir ourselves to make necessary changes. When life is too easy, we are apt to forget our true Selves and our purpose for living, lulled as we are into a state of forgetfulness. When life becomes difficult and we cannot solve our problems, we can either give up helplessly, and even be driven by despair to suicide, or call on the High C for help.

It is advisable for children to be taught from the very beginning of their lives that there is a wise, loving force within them to whom they can turn for help in times of trouble. Then they will never be reduced to the pathetic state in which so many people find themselves, of feeling rudderless and adrift on the rough ocean of life without a compass. They should not only be taught that this help is close to hand and always available but, by our example, we can show them how to find help. Only then can they develop into secure adults with the knowledge that they need never feel alone, deserted or rejected.

Why are we here at this time in history, as either a man or a woman, in this particular body, born into this family, with its particular heritage? So many seekers in the past have asked this question and sought answers in many different places and from many different people. Only the High C knows. It is only by consulting It that we can gradually become conscious of the reasons for our being in this life.

In the inner work in which I have been involved for many years, whenever I have consulted the High C on a vast and diverse variety of subjects, It has always provided answers. In addition, It has provided the material set forth in the first two books as well as this one. I have also been given insight into the many reasons for which we are in this life, and how our particular life can provide us with exactly what we need to enable us to learn from our experiences.

Our many lives can be likened to steps on a long journey back to reunion with the High C. In the overall evolutionary process, we are learning, one small step at a time, with the help of the High C, to lift ourselves up from the instinctive level of existence which we share with all living species. Our goal is union with the God-self, from which we were all originally separated, to become conscious of who we really are: a fragment of divinity.

In each lifetime, we have either moved ahead on the evolutionary path or slipped back, according to how we spent each lifetime, that is, how we acted, spoke, thought and felt and, most of all, whether we expressed love through any of those channels.

Each new life is built on the foundations of previous ones and is controlled by the High C, the sole, constant and continuous core of all the lives. Our task is to work within the evolutionary cycle into which we are born each time. In this present period, we are being given the opportunity to balance the male and female aspects within us, as they are also slowly being brought into balance in the world.

The yin and yang, or female and male, can be likened to the heart and the brain. Both are necessary to sustain life. We are all faced with the urgent need to rescue the heart, subjugated by the brain, to bring about a balance of the two in our lives and, thence, in the world. When they are balanced, we can sustain the potent energy of the High C as it takes over our lives directing us towards our goal: reunion with It. The only effective way to achieve this goal is to incur no further karma, good or bad. The only way that is possible is to defer to the High C in thought, word, feeling and act. But, if we allow the ego, with its multitudes of desires, to lure us into following its will in lieu of the superior direction of the High C, we delay our journey homeward. We have already done so in our many previous lives, or we would not have returned to be given a new opportunity to become free in this life.

Since reunion with the High C is the only reason for rebirth, we need to know if our life-style is conducive to progress or regression. This is our responsibility, whatever our age. It is never too late to make progress.

Many people ask if it is necessary to recall past lives. I can only speak for myself. For me, it has been a great help in understanding many things about my present life. But, I feel that this is the only valid reason for recovering them. Since the layers obstructing our progress have accumulated through past lives, in addition to this one, it is sometimes helpful to discover what we did in the past to delay our development. We enter each new life mercifully ignorant of all previous ones. If we did bring back memories of them all, we would be so burdened by how much we still need to learn that we would probably balk even at attempting it.

I have not always been open to the concepts of reincarnation and karma. In fact, I used to feel a great deal of opposition to them and would argue against them at every opportunity. It was not until I read about Edgar Cayce and his work that I began to open my mind to the possibility. But not until I had experienced for myself what I have slowly come to believe may have been memories of past lives was I finally willing to give serious consideration to the concept. As I look back, I realise that my change of attitude was due to the extraordinarily strong and vivid emotions accompanying my experiments in this area. These made me wonder if there might be more truth in the theory than I had been willing to believe.

When the problems people face do not seem to have a cause in this life, there is the possibility that they could have originated in one or more past-life experiences. If this seems to be the case, it is often advisable to travel back in time to try to discover the root cause of the problem and, thereby, the lesson for the present life.

I am never directed to regress people into past lives if they are seeking such experiences out of idle curiosity. Neither do I attempt to take a person back on such a quest unless it has been made very clear by the High C that it is timely for that particular person to do so, and that regression will help him to live his present life with more understanding.

Various signs usually indicate the need to seek in past lives the solutions to present problems. Sometimes, people have vague memories of being someone other than their present personality. When they are offered a way to clarify their impressions, they are usually greatly relieved, especially if they have been afraid to mention them for fear of being thought crazy. Other people may have a very strong intimation of having lived in another country which they have never knowingly visited. Some report that they had strong feelings, either positive or negative, about a country or city they visited. They describe how they were able to recognise landmarks and knew exactly the route to take to reach certain places, as only a resident would normally be able to do. For some people, the art or music of another culture holds a strong attraction, or a particular language will be very easy for them to learn. Still others have recurring dreams of a place they have not visited. These are a few of the many signs which indicate that the memories of a possible past experience appear to be nearer to the surface of consciousness than is usual.

There are also myriads of congenital sicknesses and deformities which defy explanation if viewed only in terms of the present existence. These can be better understood and, sometimes, resolved when their possible origin in a past life is discovered.

Many such hints can be of great help in guiding a person back to a specific place or time. However, it must be emphasised that by asking for direction from the High C, nothing that is too difficult or painful for the person to accept or handle will be uncovered. Those rather dubious stories of past lives as famous people are rarely experienced. Most of the lives people describe are of ordinary people with the usual humdrum problems. Now and then, a more dramatic one will emerge, particularly if the former personality lived during a war. Hundreds of Cleopatras, Napoleons, Nefertitis and other historical figures have supposedly been the past personalities of many people who have been regressed. Unfortunately, these claims cast doubt on the whole subject. A serious problem is created when people prefer to bask in the reflected glory of real or imagined past fame and achievement instead of concentrating on living fully in the present.

Each life can be likened to a facet of the whole Self, just as a diamond has many facets hidden within the rough stone. Only the gem-cutter can reveal the hidden beauty with his cutting and polishing tools. Each life offers the opportunity to have a new facet polished by a return to a new human body. The way the person lives his life and the quality of his relationships help in the polishing. Finally, after many earth experiences, the whole diamond will be cut and polished so that every facet reflects the light of the High C, who is also the gem-cutter. Unfortunately, we rarely co-operate with that superior aspect within us and, therefore, make it very difficult for It to cut and shape us as only It knows how to do.

It has been repeatedly impressed upon me that only this present life is important. Only in the present are we able to surrender our wills to that of the High C and co-operate willingly and consciously in the moulding process designed for the present living personality.

In some people's lives, the task or lesson they are here to learn is so obvious that they have no need to search for the answer to the age-old question, 'Why am I here?' They arrived on earth knowing why. There are others, however, who cannot see clearly the pattern, goal or reason for their life. Consequently, they live an aimless existence, lacking direction or incentive. In such cases, it is often extremely helpful for them to journey back to a past experience which may help to focus on a specific area of the old personality which still needs to be worked on.

Past lives have also created various roles, some of which have been brought over as habits into the present. If the memory of the original role carries strong enough emotional energy, that is usually sufficient to bring it back as a vague memory, triggered by events in the current life. If we think back in our present life and try to remember a specific event, those occurrences that carry a strong charge of emotional energy come to mind easily and quickly. An exception would be an experience containing an emotional reaction that was too powerful or upsetting. In that case, the entire episode might be suppressed. Such is often the case with incest or sexual abuse.

So, it is as if we still carry traces of our past personalities in addition to our present one. Until we are aware of the need to re-educate those parts of ourselves, it is useless for others to bring them to our attention. We would merely discount their view as imagination, naïveté, spite, jealousy or egotism. Only when we are fully aware of both our positive and negative aspects are we in a position to surrender all of our selves to the High C for Its direction.

For those who find this whole concept of past lives difficult to accept, an alternative approach can be taken in which each episode is seen as a teaching story similar to those used by the Sufis. It is the underlying teaching that is important rather than whether the episode is actually a past life. Viewed in this way, the main character could represent a facet of a person, very much as the characters appearing in dreams often symbolise aspects of the dreamer's own personality. Such stories can just as easily be used to point out areas needing healing or change, which is the only useful purpose for delving into the self at all. The important point to bear in mind is the quest for self-knowledge, not proof of past lives.

There are many different methods that are now popular for taking people back into former incarnations. However, the motive should not be to identify with famous characters and then try to live in their reflected glory, as some people have done. We should revive old memories only if, in so doing, we are helped to live our present life with more awareness.

If, by going back in memory, we see more clearly what we have set in motion, the results of which we are facing now, then it can be very helpful. For it can enable us to try consciously to correct old errors, make amends for past wrongs, or experience for ourselves what we formerly meted out to others so that we can learn, by suffering as they did, where we went wrong.

Chapter 29

PAST LIVES

In this chapter I will share some of my own experiences to show how they have affected my present life, sometimes positively, and at other times negatively. Each past-life session was always preceded by a very strong emotion, positive or negative, often starting several days before the actual experience and heightened by vivid dreams. Eventually, I learned that to break through the control of the conscious mind, strong emotional energy is necessary, just as our most vivid memories in this life are those in which a strong emotion was experienced.

The Persian Woman

Before my very first regression, I was haunted by the fear that I would not be able to succeed in recalling any past experiences simply because I had never been able to visualise anything. For instance, if I looked carefully at my husband or my two daughters and closed my eyes, I could not recreate their likeness in my mind's eye, however hard I tried. So, I truly dreaded that first session and, had my desire to understand my present life not been so intense, I doubt that I could have attempted to investigate the past. The fear increased as I was being relaxed by the man who was introducing me to this method. As soon as he directed me to go back in memory to a past experience, I panicked. Though I knew I was becoming aware of somewhere different from the room in which the session was taking place, for the life of me, I could not tell him anything I was seeing, however much he questioned me. Finally, he suggested that I use one of my other senses and asked what I could hear, smell or feel.

At that suggestion, I decided to move around the space I felt I was in, with my hands held out in front of me. In this way, it seemed as if my fingers came in contact with a texture that felt exactly like a carpet. But, instead of being on the ground, it was upright. I moved around the space in a circle and discovered several similar carpets, apparently hanging around the walls of the enclosure in which I was standing. They slightly overlapped and I could feel the edges where they came together. After a while, I arrived at an open space where they ended. I continued on past it and again felt more carpets, so I knew I must have passed the entrance to the place I was in. Suddenly, it dawned on me that I was blind. With that realisation, a veritable torrent of pent-up emotion was released in tears. I understood then that I must have brought over from this experience into my present life my supersensitive eyes.

In a later session, I went further back in the same life to a time before I became blind. I discovered that it had taken place in Persia. The woman with whom I had identified myself was the wife of a man attached to the court of one of the many minor kingdoms which was ruled by a powerful woman. When the wife had inadvertently discovered a dark secret about this ruler, she was ordered to be blinded and banished. She was found by a band of travelling gypsy shepherds who took her with them and looked after her until she had recovered from her ordeal. Without sight, she was forced to rely more heavily on her other senses, which became more acute with the added burden placed upon them. She also relied on her intuition, one of her naturally strong functions. In time, she became the advisor, or oracle, of the band. The members appealed to her for help and advice in solving their individual problems as well as those of the group. The enclosure, lined with hanging carpets, was one of the tents they carried with them when they travelled and set up wherever they decided to camp.

Several years after this recall, my husband and I visited Iran on a business trip. One day, we were driven outside Teheran into the surrounding countryside. As we drove along, off to the left of the road, we saw dozens of strange-looking circular tents being dismantled by a band of gypsies. They were busily packing up their temporary camp before travelling on their way to other pastures. I reacted with strong emotion as I watched, fascinated, when they lifted down the carpets which had been hanging on the inside of the tents, folded them neatly, and stacked them on the backs of their pack animals. It was all exactly as I had experienced in the reverie many years earlier.

I remember having been extremely sceptical at the time I recalled this life, but the strong emotions which flooded through me again when I saw the actual scene taking place before my physical eyes, made me more open to accepting it as likely.

From early childhood, I have always been more than ordinarily sensitive to all external stimuli, such as loud noises, bright lights, strong tastes and smells, as well as more subtle ones. All my senses seem to be attuned to a higher pitch than normal, which I was better able to understand after I had experienced this recall. It also helped to explain why, all my life, people have brought their problems to me. By losing my sight in the Persian life, I had gained other aptitudes and turned what could easily have been a disaster into an opportunity for service.

The Japanese Girl

Another experience, which illustrates how we often bring back old patterns, abilities and talents from the past into the present, took place in Japan. Many of the details were again corroborated much later during my first visit to that country. The first session was also preceded by strong emotions a few days before its commencement.

Ever since I could remember, heights had frightened me. This fear, together with an extra sensitivity, were greatly accentuated for several days before the next session and even more so immediately before I arrived for the regression appointment. As soon as I closed my eyes, the emotions became so overpowering that I was catapulted into the experience before I had time to be relaxed. I immediately recalled a terror I had suffered as a small child living in England. I was haunted by a fear of earthquakes. My parents tried to reassure me by saying that earthquakes were unheard of in England, but to no avail. I kept repeating over and over, that I knew they could happen, and so unexpectedly that people would be too surprised to have time to save themselves. When asked how I knew, I always said I remembered it had happened, which agitated my parents even more. I was now extremely eager to discover the origin of this fear. I had not yet learned to use the triangle and the High C but, even then, I was aware that I could make contact with a teaching-force within me, so I appealed to It for guidance and help.

I soon became aware of a scene which reminded me of a Japanese landscape, except that I felt in some strange way that I was part of it. I consciously allowed myself to move into the scene and became so immersed in it that I felt I was actually there. Everything felt very real to me, much more so than my own physical body and its surroundings during the session. As in a play, various scenes unfolded. I identified myself with a young Japanese girl who was excited and expectant, like a child anticipating a special treat. I began to experience everything from then on as if I were this young girl. Occasionally, I separated myself from her and returned to my present identity, to evaluate something I was experiencing, when directed to do so by my inner guide. I felt as if I were shuffling from room to room, inspecting a house situated on high ground overlooking the sea. It was surrounded by meticulously maintained gardens planted in such a way that each small part was a separate garden within the main one, each one laid out in a different style. A small summer teahouse stood at the edge of the gardens overlooking a harbour.

The girl was dressed in an elaborate kimono of lacquer-red silk, tied with an ornate *obi*, or sash, both obviously chosen with great care. I knew she was awaiting a man with whom she had fallen in love. He was expected to arrive that day by ship, so she wanted everything to be in perfect order for the meeting. After her tour of inspection, she went to a room with a shrine at one end. On a mat on the floor beneath the shrine, a pile of branches and flowers had been laid. After making a quick little bow towards the shrine, she started to sort out the branches and place them carefully in a shallow bowl on a small wooden table. She chose very carefully from the pile, selecting several boughs and snipping off twigs here and there, until the shapes satisfied her. She then began to set them into the bowl in a deliberate fashion. I sensed a twinge of guilt and became aware that she was placing one branch in an incorrect position in relation to the others. It symbolised for her the man she loved. She placed it in the central position of the arrangement, more prominently than the one symbolising the Unknown, or Spirit. When she had completed the arrangement, she reached into the folds of her obi and took out a small wooden object which just fitted into the palm of her hand. She opened it by pulling on two door-like panels to reveal a tiny shrine containing a miniature carved figure of the Buddha standing under a canopy. She sat holding it, meditating for while, her lips moving slightly as if intoning a mantra or prayer. After a few minutes, she closed it and slipped it back inside her obi.

As she sat quietly, I became aware of her thoughts and was able to piece together her story. She was the daughter of a wealthy merchant who traded with foreign countries. Her mother had died, leaving her the mistress of the house. Her father was expecting a visit from an important representative of a firm with which he dealt almost exclusively, and who came periodically for business meetings. The two men had developed a closer relationship than was usual under such circumstances, so the visitor had been extended the rare privilege of being invited to the house on several occasions. During these visits, a wordless communication had developed between him and the daughter of the house and it was he whom she now so eagerly awaited. Her father was only vaguely aware of this situation. He did not take it seriously for the simple reason that a husband had already been selected for his daughter and the marriage date set. So he was unconcerned, so certain was he that their meetings could never be a serious threat to these arrangements. Taking advantage of his unconcern, they met secretly in the garden. There was a serious language barrier. Each had picked up a few words with which to communicate, in addition to sign language. The man's pet name for her was 'Aspen Leaf', which he felt suited her sensitive nature so well. Her every move reminded him of the fluttering leaves of the aspen trees in the garden where they walked.

After meditating with the aid of her hand-shrine, she made her way out of the house. She stole swiftly through the formal gardens and into the summer house where she had a clear view of the harbour and all the ships sailing in, one of which would soon bring her beloved. She had just slipped into the garden when a wrenching sound tore its tranquil atmosphere. The ground shook as an earthquake hit the area. The teahouse was hurled over the edge of the cliff and down on to the ground far below, carrying her in it. As she hit the ground, her spirit was shaken free from her crushed body. She could still see it clothed in the beautiful kimono, though she did not understood what had happened. Her only thought was to stay near the kimono-clad body to ensure that she would not miss her beloved.

At this point, I began to recognise how, in this present life, I too possessed a very sensitive nature. I had also put those I loved ahead of the High C. As a child, I had suffered great fear, both of earthquakes and of heights. But it was not until much later, when I became involved in the present work, that I was shown how to be free of these problems.

Several years after recalling this life, I accompanied my husband on a trip to Japan. While we were there, I had several strange experiences. For me, they corroborated many of the puzzling details I had uncovered during this session. I experienced my first shock when we visited Kyoto and entered a little antique shop that reeked of opium. For no conscious reason, I walked directly to the back of the shop, reached up and to the back of a high shelf and brought down in my hand a small object I had found there. To my utter amazement, it was a tiny shrine exactly like the one I had seen the Japanese girl take out of her obi in my reverie many years earlier. My whole body trembled as I held it in my hand. In my present life, I had never seen one before and, at the time I had recalled the Japanese life, I had doubted that such a thing existed, being certain that I had imagined it. Of course, we bought the shrine and asked the old shopkeeper to tell us more about it. He told us that it was called a hand-shrine and they were kept in a lady's obi when not being held in the hand during meditation exactly as I had seen in my inner experience years before.

A few days later, I was fortunate enough to be invited to join a class for prospective brides being conducted by a master in the art of flower arrangement. Our interpreter explained that attendance at these classes was one of several premarital requirements for young Japanese girls. I was excited and delighted to be allowed to participate. We were each given a pile of branches, a pair of clippers and a flower container. The old master first demonstrated an arrangement before the class. He showed us how to choose the branches, shape them and place them in the correct order, just as I had observed during my regression. We were then told to recreate the arrangement with our own pile of branches. As we all started to snip and cut, I found that my fingers seemed to know just what to do. The master was obviously surprised at the result and bowed several times, not to me, but to the arrangement. I left the lesson in a daze caused by both recognition and disbelief.

My next shock came when we took a drive to an old residential area built on high land overlooking the sea outside Tokyo. A chill ran down my spine when we came to an area reminiscent of the place where the Japanese girl had lived. I asked our guide if there were any aspen trees nearby. He immediately pointed out several as we drove along the road!

Just before we were to leave Japan, my husband's Japanese clients sent around to our hotel a large, gaily wrapped box addressed to me. I opened it and, to my very great surprise, found inside a gorgeous kimono of lacquer-red silk embroidered with silver cranes. I was thankful that I was alone when I opened it. The shock of being given a kimono of the very same colour as the one the Japanese girl had worn at her death would have been too much to handle in front of the kind donors. (Cranes, incidentally, are symbols of a happy marriage.)

A little later, on that same trip, we flew to Cambodia to see the famous Angkor Watt. As we wandered around the various other watts, our guide indicated a small temple at the top of a steep flight of steps. He told us that it housed a particularly beautiful figure of the Buddha. I badly wanted to climb up to see it but, because of my fear of heights, I was afraid that if I went up I would be too frightened to come down again. So I decided to wait below while my husband and the guide climbed up. As I sat at the base of the temple, my desire to see the statue of the Buddha intensified. At the same time, the memory of the Japanese girl came to my mind. Suddenly, I had the idea to imagine taking her by the hand and leading her up the steps to the top. I hesitated at the thought, but found the courage to climb a step at a time. As I climbed, I kept mentally reassuring her that she need have no fear. In this way, I soon reached the top, to the amazement and concern of my husband. After seeing the statue, I still had the return descent to manage and, with that realisation, came another rush of fear. I persuaded my husband to go down ahead of me with the guide and assured him that I would follow when I was ready. He reluctantly acquiesced. I sat for a while quietly talking to the Japanese girl as if she were a frightened child beside me. I finally stood up and, taking her firmly by the hand, went slowly down that steep flight of steps, being very careful not to look down. When I reached the ground, I was jubilant at having succeeded in overcoming my fear. Since then, I have not experienced the old terror and have climbed up and down high places many times without fear. I have also become less like an aspen leaf reacting to every little breeze. But, even more important, I have learned never to place a human being above the High C.

The Jew

Another probable past life which has a bearing on my present one was that of a Jew living in an area that is now Jerusalem. I tuned into him on his death-bed, as he lay helplessly paralysed, desperate to be free of his useless body. As I allowed myself to merge with him, I became aware that he had lived a life dedicated to 'wine, women and song', until his body had rebelled at the excesses he had forced it to experience. I was afraid that this might be a figment of my imagination as it did not seem at all probable that a Jew would forsake the dictates of his religion to such an extent. I continued to alternate between observing and experiencing him until death finally released him, and his spirit flew free of his body. He had plenty of time to repent his wasted life and, as he escaped, he swore that he would never again repeat that pattern.

His vow rang true for me in this life. Wherever possible, I have always avoided any gatherings such as cocktail parties, where people were likely to drink too much. I particularly dislike typical New Year's Eve celebrations. I am also allergic to all alcohol, even wine. My liver is very easily upset, perhaps another pattern brought over from the past life of over-indulgence, now acting as a built-in protection against repeating the excesses.

At least ten years after I had experienced this recall, I read a book entitled *Jews, God and History* by Max Dimont. One passage in it gave me real jolt. The author described the effect of the Greek culture and its practices on some groups of Jews in a certain period, and referred to them as Hellenised Jews.

Dimont wrote that, between AD 700 and 1000, Jews became cosmopolitan, and began to translate many Greek works. The Jew of that time differed from the biblical Jew by becoming 'a hedonist and philanderer, a bon vivant and sophisticate, a worldly philosopher and scientist, a secular writer and poet. Wine was not only a drink for benediction, but a toast to a woman's lips; love meant not only the study of the Torah, but also the pursuit of a promising smile; song was not only a lamentation, but also a paeon to the joy of life.'

This helped to dispel yet another of my doubts about the authenticity of the lives I had uncovered, as this description so exactly described the kind of life I had glimpsed in the recall, that I no longer doubted it, nor thought it a figment of my imagination.

The Tibetan

Another possible past experience, as a Tibetan monk, also shed light on my present life. In the recall, I had the impression that the monk was under the tutelage and personal direction of a Master, or High Lama. A telepathic connection had been intentionally developed between them, preparatory to a period of three years, three months, three weeks and three days, during which time the monk was voluntarily sealed into a cave high in the Himalayas for a special meditational practice. As a disciple following his Master's direction, he had allowed himself to be closed into the cave for the specific purpose of relinquishing his desires. These included desires for specific things, both tangible and mental, as well as the desire that certain events should not take place. He had been carefully prepared by his Master. At first, in personal meetings, the Master had directed him to practise a set of exercises in non-attachment. Later, as they became better attuned, the teaching was continued telepathically.

When I recalled this life, I entered it at the point when the monk had been in the cave for more than two years, and had developed the ability to see with the third eye. With practice, when his eyes were closed, a small screen appeared in the middle of his forehead on which symbols of conscious desire were projected. As long as he kept in close touch with the Master, the latter was able to direct the input according to the pupil's growing ability to handle it. He was taught to allow a desire or fear (in symbolic form) to be introduced on to the inner mental screen. Its strength was in direct proportion to the amount of energy he had invested in it. At the height of its power, he was instructed to imagine he was squeezing out all the energy or emotion contained in the symbol and then destroying the remaining empty shell or husk. Sometimes, it would take weeks to de-energise a strong wish or desire. Other desires might be easier to dispel, but might then reappear in a slightly different form, or on another level of awareness.

He had absolute faith in his Master, but no concept of any greater authority beyond him, either inside or outside himself. One day, the connection between them suddenly began to fade until it finally broke off altogether. Without supervision, he was inundated by the thought-forms and fears pouring into his mind in a merciless torrent. He was incapable of coping with them on his own. If he had been aware of the High C, he could have immediately called on It for help. However, as the Lama had taught him to rely solely on him, when their telepathic link was severed, he was driven to madness by the invasion of thought-forms. Finally, in desperation, he banged his head against the wall of the cave to stop the flow of images. His skull was fractured, which eventually led to his death. So, in one sense, he had committed suicide.

Naturally, after uncovering this sequence of events, I was curious to discover what had happened to break the telepathic connection between the monk and his Master. I was shown a festival in progress at which the High Lama was to officiate. He was borne aloft through the crowds on a palanquin carried on the shoulders of younger lamas. The revelry of the lay people rose to such a pitch that, in the ensuing fracas, he was jostled and fell, striking his head when he hit the ground. He was temporarily unconscious, which broke the telepathic connection to his pupil. When he regained consciousness, he hastily sought a reconnection, but by then it was too late.

This episode illustrates two important lessons: the necessity for maintaining contact with the High C even when one has a revered human teacher; and the warning that no matter how desperate a situation becomes, taking one's own life is not a solution. It merely defers the problem to a future life when a similar though often more serious dilemma will arise requiring resolution. Every problem must be handled with courage, so that the lesson it contains can be learned. The first lesson was failed in both the Japanese and Tibetan lives for, in both, a human being was given more importance than the High C. The second lesson was failed in the Jewish and Tibetan lives, as they both sought to escape their problems in death.

In this present life, I have again been faced with the opportunity to learn both these lessons.

My past-life recalls took place many years before I read about Sai Baba in 1972 and went to India the following year to meet him. I still vividly recall that first visit and the battle which raged in me as I sat in his presence, wrestling with the deep-seated fear of relying on a teacher in human form. Baba, in his own inimitable way, was aware of my dilemma and darted glances in my direction from time to time. He wove into his talk to the group of guests little hints designed to help me, and smiled as if to say, 'Yes, I know! Does this help?' This situation continued for days, until he delivered a talk to the teachers and college students and gave my husband and me permission to attend it.

In his talk, he elaborated on the subject of idol worship and discussed the various world religions. He stressed the point that everyone is at different levels of understanding. Some need a tangible idol to remind them of God; others need many different forms, each representing a certain quality or aspect of God, as in Hinduism. Only a few are able to comprehend an abstract, formless deity, or seek contact with the God-within, the *Ātman*, the Christ-self. This explanation took care of my problem, I suddenly understood that Baba was the personification in human form of the High C, the spark of truth within me.

Just before we left, he materialised a ring for me, to cure one of the causes of my headaches. He put it on the first finger of my left hand, and told me to rub it on the middle of my forehead whenever it hurt there. As he slipped it on my finger, the memory of the Tibetan life flashed into my mind. I gasped, 'Oh Baba!' He smiled, nodded and answered, 'Yes, yes I know all about it. This will help to heal it.'

At our farewell interview, I asked Baba when we should return. He pointed at me with the index finger of his right hand to emphasise his words and said, 'First, understand that you do not need to come back to see this little body,' indicating himself. After a significant pause, he continued: 'Find me in your heart.' After another pause, to allow his message to penetrate, he continued, 'But you will come back to be re-energised.'

In similar ways, he has given me short but powerful messages each time we have visited him. Also, without actually putting it in words, he has made me understand that he is fully aware of my past as well as my present experiences. He helps without taking away the opportunity to absorb the various lessons this life has to offer. By only giving hints, he forces us to find the answers from within ourselves, from the High C. He is like a Zen master who gives a student a koan, or riddle, on which to work, to occupy his conscious mind so completely that in its efforts to solve the koan it is diverted sufficiently to allow the High C to break through with true insights. For me, Baba has become more and more an outer symbol of the indwelling God. He has accelerated my learning, but never, at any time, has he allowed me to become dependent on his physical form, as did the Tibetan lama with his disciple in the cave.

A Life at the Time of Jesus

A life at the time of Jesus was retrieved in an unexpected way when I was not consciously seeking such an experience. On the contrary, I was working with a woman who hoped to be able to retrieve one of her past lives. She had had intimations of a life lived at the time of Jesus' ministry. She also felt that she had known Paul of Tarsus. We asked the High C if it would be beneficial for her to try to uncover the origin of her feelings related to the period.

As soon as we started to work, she became aware of another time and place and of herself as a different personality from her present one. I gently prodded her with questions to help with the recall. She reported seeing and feeling herself as a little girl living with a group of people. As she brought to consciousness more details from her far memory, without any warning, I seemed suddenly to have entered the scene with her at a point when she was describing a large room containing a group of people all busily weaving. This was the very first time I had ever intruded uninvited, into another person's past-life recall. It happened so quickly and unexpectedly that it was quite startling to both of us.

At first, I was not sure whether I was a man or a woman. This confusion was soon explained when it became clear that we belonged to a group who all wore very similar simple white garments and had their heads covered, so it was difficult to differentiate between men and women. I eventually identified myself with a man who at first seemed to be an overseer; soon it became evident that he was more like an orchestra conductor. He set the tone for the workers by intoning a chant to help them work rhythmically and therefore more efficiently. When I asked the High C why this scene had evoked such a dramatic response in me, the answer came to my mind very strongly, that the garments being woven were to be worn by Jesus. A special chant, or mantra, was being intoned which carried a strong emotional energy. This practice always accompanied the process of weaving, as well as all the other handicrafts, to bless the work, similar to the practice of saying grace before eating.

I watched as the man left the weaving room and made the rounds of the many other groups who were making pottery, preparing food while others cooked it, baking bread, cleaning, washing clothes, tending the gardens, and engaged in all the other necessary tasks of a community wherein everyone had a given role.

The next scene described by the woman with whom I was working was quite obviously at a later time. She sensed a heavy cloud of depression that seemed to hang over the community. We both instinctively knew that she was witnessing the period immediately following the crucifixion of Jesus. The little girl she had seen earlier was now a young woman. She and the man with whom I had identified myself, and many others, appeared confused and disappointed. They found it hard to believe that Jesus had allowed himself to be killed, thereby deserting them. They felt deceived, betrayed and, even worse, lost without a leader.

An even later scene revealed the man furtively making his way in and out of the narrow streets of a city, repeatedly looking around, to be sure he was not being followed. He would turn the wrong way now and then, or make a wide detour to confuse anyone trying to follow him. I gathered that he was protecting the dwindling number of survivors of the original band of friends and followers of Jesus. He had apparently hidden them from their enemies. He took his job very seriously and suffered terribly whenever news of each new death reached him, or when a member of his little flock, who had managed to escape, sought refuge under his roof and brought news of fresh horrors perpetrated by their enemies.

In this life, too, a pattern similar to the one in the Japanese and Tibetan lives can be recognised. Though Jesus is the Son of God to many, the faith of these people, who relied on him so completely, was obviously imperfect or insufficient, thus rendering their plight after his crucifixion identical to that of someone dependent on a human personality: they were utterly bereft after his death.

It is apparent from the many sayings attributed to Jesus that he tried to teach them that it was 'The Father within that doeth the works,' such as miracles and healings. He also told them that they could do likewise if they turned within and allowed the Father to perform his works through them. However, when he was no longer physically present to remind them, they forgot his words and lamented his departure, having longingly projected on to him their own Father-within or the High C, instead of seeking It within themselves, as in, 'The Kingdom of Heaven is within.'

This particular past life also explained some of my very early negative reactions to Christianity. I was often told that, as a small child, I had announced one day that I did not think it was fair to expect me to be perfect like Jesus. He was God, whereas I was only a little girl. It was also reported to me that I had often said that I could not understand why people who went to church were kind and good only on Sundays, but the opposite on other days of the week.

Another lifelong puzzle has been my complete lack of any sense of direction. Invariably, I turn in the opposite direction to the one I should be taking to reach my destination. I now realised that this could be due to an extreme caution brought over from the latter part of the early Christian life, when it was my task to protect the surviving followers of Jesus. An excessively strong reaction to the death of anyone with whom I have been deeply involved, especially in this work, might also have originated in that life. Fortunately, understanding the likely origin of such emotions has allowed me to release these patterns, and to realise that I am not responsible for the life or death of anyone, since each has his own destiny which no one can circumvent or prevent.

Lextra

All the above lives and several others, including the present one, have been overshadowed by one very powerful male personality who appeared to live very far back in time. One day, I found myself about to enter a life that felt so foreign to my present personality that I immediately retreated out of stark fear. Eventually, I realised that I needed to discover why I was so afraid to uncover it, so I proceeded to bring back one tiny segment at a time until a more complete picture of the life was revealed. The essence of it was that this man, whose name was Lextra, had wielded an inordinate amount of power; whereas, in this present life, I have been so afraid of power that I have consistently avoided any semblance of using it, especially over other people.

As I investigated further, I could actually experience this man's powerfulness. He was determined to obtain as much knowledge as possible about the various natural laws governing the planet. He spared neither himself nor others in his quest. He was not evil, just insatiably thirsty for knowledge and the power it can bring to its possessor. His mind was overdeveloped; his heart and his ability to feel, particularly to love, were sadly deficient. So great was his compulsion to learn, that he overlooked the effect he had on others. He treated people as if they were objects instead of human beings with feelings and sensitivity. He drove them as relentlessly as he himself was driven by his lust for knowledge and power.

Quite some time after Lextra had first emerged, in another session I was shown a huge book which I later learned was a ledger listing credits and debits. On the very first page was inscribed the name of this powerful figure. It had been so heavily etched that it had actually cut into the page. As I turned more pages, one by one, the impression of the name was still clearly visible, though gradually becoming fainter, until at last, I reached a page where it was barely decipherable. I knew that I had arrived at my present life. At first, the discovery that his name was impressed onto each life upto the present one was a real shock. Then I began to realise that in each subsequent life I had recovered by regression, I had had an opportunity to compensate for Lextra's influence and, sometimes, even to erase some of the old karmic debts he had incurred. In each life, the main lesson concerned an aspect of love, the chief quality missing in this mind-dominated, power-hungry man. With that insight, I was flooded with a feeling of deep compassion, not only for him but for everyone like him. I have always sorrowed for all those people who are adept at thinking but lack the ability to express and to receive love.

I was next shown that if I were to continue to work on myself and be willing to share the learning, experiences and techniques I received with those who earnestly asked for guidance, I could, with the help of the High C, finally erase Lextra's name from the ledger. I would thus be freed from his shadow and the karmic debts I had inherited from him which have haunted each of my successive lives. I have paid dearly, not only in past lives, but also in this present one for wielding power over others and, in so doing, failing to honour their free will. The energy used to accomplish such control then has returned to me in the form of control by others, though not necessarily those I originally wronged.

It would appear that we are all woven together in one massive web. All our thoughts, words, feelings and deeds affect anyone who attracts them by their own behaviour, either past or present. So we are all both teachers and pupils of one another, since everything that happens to us offers us an opportunity to learn.

How very appropriate that I was led to Sai Baba, whose main message is, 'Start the day with love, fill the day with love, live the day with love, and end the day with love,' and who advocates using work as worship, instead of solely for self-gratification, power or financial security!

Having received such insights from researching into my own past lives it seemed only natural for me to want to help others to unearth experiences that could give them insights into their present life's problems and relationships. However, I have been instructed to do this only if so directed by the High C.

Sometimes a person will be led back into a past experience in the middle of a routine reverie session. In that case, the facilitator needs to question him very carefully in order to elicit the main lesson still to be learned from that life. It is altogether too easy to get lost in the drama, scenery, glamour, or extraordinarily strong emotions being evoked and to miss the chief point of the lesson to be learned, or the warning being given. These lessons are the only authentic reasons for reviewing past lives.

Not everyone is able to go back in time. Some people block the recall for a reason. If it seems likely that a person's particular problem stems from a former life's experience, another worker may offer to go back into the past to seek the cause if he is directed to do so by the High C. Sometimes a pair of people working together report their findings to a person either by letter or by a telephone call.

Many such lives have been recovered in this way, and almost always the stories strike a responsive note in the person who has asked for this service. It is always fascinating when attitudes, habits, fears, likes and dislikes which could not possibly have been known about someone are revealed in past-life stories. It is also heart-warming to watch old fears disappear when their original cause is known. Not knowing the reason for a reaction is one of the most difficult aspects of any problem. When the origin is uncovered, the problem can usually be worked out.

Two of the most common problems that appear to have their origin in a past life are sexual frigidity and fear of sex. Many times we have uncovered cases of rape in a past life which have cast their shadow onto the lives of present personalities. These unconscious memories have often prevented the unfortunate person from being free to express love and willingly participate in the sexual aspect of a relationship.

Quite often, very close relationships are clarified when a member of the present family is identified as having been a member of an earlier family in a past experience, but in a different relationship from the present one. Thus, a father in this life may have been a brother, uncle, or son before, or even a female relative. A person's eyes seem to carry his identity. Indeed, the eyes have been called 'windows to the soul'. So I always suggest that the person retrieving past memories look at the eyes of the people appearing in his inner picture to see if they remind him of anyone in his present life. It seems that the eyes carry a constant identity.

Each person carries within him a series of life-stories, all different from those belonging to anyone else. It is best for each person to ask to be shown which of his own past experiences will be most helpful for him to uncover, rather than to try to copy or identify himself with those that others have retrieved. If such research into the past is carried out under the guidance of the High C, only those experiences that are useful now will be brought into the conscious mind for digestion/absorbtion

I cannot stress too strongly the absolute necessity to cut the ties to each life recovered. This can be done by using the same technique as described earlier with parents and others. When this is done, many fears, habits, ailments and other problems stemming from past life experiences are released. This erases their stamp on the form of the present life.

Another very necessary warning entails bringing the regressed person back to full consciousness of his present body at the present time, date and place at the end of each session. I have worked with many people who had been taken back by someone else to a past experience, both individually and as part of a group regression, but have not been brought back to full awareness of their present. Some of them have told me that they have felt as if they were not completely back in their body. Others have suffered the even more serious reaction of continuing to have a negative overlay from the past life superimposed on the present one, causing great confusion. Such problems are usually the result of regressions undertaken without the help of the High C.

It is also essential for the person retrieving past lives to ask the High C the following questions:

- What did I learn from that life?

- Did I progress or regress?

- What do I still need to learn that my present life can make possible?

- What physical or psychological problems were brought over into the present life?

- What fears, habits or attitudes were initiated in the past?

- What roles from the past do I still need to release?

The answers to these questions will give a clearer view of what needs to be accomplished this time around.

In each life, we merely borrow for an unknown length of time the various things we need and the people with whom we will have close relationships, both positive and negative. By becoming too closely attached to anything or anyone, we create bonds for ourselves and others. If people have cut the ties to anyone or anything that controls them and have remained free from further excessively constricting attachments, they will be free at the time of death to relinquish the physical body and everyone and everything attaching them to it during this lifetime. They can then experience a conscious death during which they will discover that they are still very much alive but, having escaped from the confinement of their physical body, are freed from its restraints. They can then follow the bright guiding light that will lead them beyond this dimension to a different and lighter mode of existence in a less dense, more fluid form or body. Contact is frequently made with family members or loved ones who have already left the world of form. They can act as a welcoming committee to help to guide newcomers into the mode of existence so very different from the one they are leaving. When the death is conscious, that is, when the dying person is not medically drugged, sedated, or in a coma, they can often describe the other-worldly music they are hearing, the extraordinary colours they are seeing and the joy they can feel at the prospect of reunion with loved ones gathered to welcome them beyond the threshold of death.

However, sometimes the reverse is the case. The dying person may be afraid to die, reluctant to leave people or things to which he is unduly attached. Or he may even be afraid of meeting deceased family members for unknown personal reasons. In such instances, it is possible to call on others who are no longer in physical form, and who have undertaken to guide those who need help to move beyond the pull of earth's gravity into the new dimension with which they themselves have had time to become familiar. They act as a spiritual midwife and supervise the 'birth' into another dimension, a new way of life.

Chapter 30

DREAMS

Long before I began to receive this method of working, I once heard someone remark that a person undergoing Freudian, Jungian or any other psychological therapy, would dream according to how that particular discipline interpreted dreams. At the time, I scoffed at this idea.

Since then, I have had to eat my own words, as they say. During many counselling sessions I have discovered that, despite how they have dreamed before, people start to dream in a way that enables me to help them understand the messages contained in their dreams. It is as if the subconscious mind becomes aware that its messages will be understood if it produces dreams the therapist can help to interpret by the method in use.

Sometimes, I meet a person who announces with great conviction that he never dreams. This statement cannot be correct. Everyone dreams, but not everyone remembers their dreams upon awakening.

Many dream clinics have sprung up in recent years to do research into dreams and dreaming. One of the discoveries is that REMS (rapid eye movements) indicate when a sleeper is dreaming. Because dreams so often evaporate like snow in the sunlight, a method has been suggested to facilitate their retention. It entails waking the person being tested as soon as the REMS are detected. He is then asked to relate the dream he was just witnessing. With such assistance, those who have, until then, not been able to remember their dreams at all can recount them in great detail. But not everyone can undergo such a stringent test. So an easy method is needed to help people to remember their dreams, a method that could become a regular habit. For instance, very few people seem to be aware that they can ask for a dream to help them solve a problem, or throw light on a situation needing clarification. This knowledge provides many people with a sufficiently strong incentive to retrieve their dreams and awaken immediately after dreaming.

Many people ask for a method of recording their dreams. I usually suggest they place a cassette player on their bedside table, close enough to be turned on as soon as they awake from a dream, to encourage them to record it while it is still fresh in their memory. It can be transcribed later, at leisure.

If the above method is not possible for some reason, such as disturbing a partner, an alternative is to place a pad of paper, or a 'dream journal', and a pen with a tiny flashlight attached to it next to the bed. This enables the dreamer to see well enough to record the dream without awakening the person sleeping nearby. Of course, if a person is sleeping alone, a small light can be turned on. However, even with such aids, many people discover, to their dismay, that they cannot read their own writing afterwards. For this reason, many people prefer to speak their dreams into a tape recorder.

I shall never forget the woman who told me that she could not recall ever having dreamed. I explained that, undoubtedly, she had always dreamed but, for some reason, was unable to remember her dreams. I asked her if she had ever consciously asked for a dream just as she was about to fall asleep. She replied that it had never occurred to her to do such a strange thing. I suggested that she might like to try a little experiment by gently but firmly giving a message to her subconscious mind that she would like to be given a dream and, furthermore, that she would like to recall it after awakening. She agreed to try, but was obviously doubtful of its success.

My telephone rang earlier than usual the next morning. When I answered it, the woman's excited voice greeted me with, 'I hope it is not too early to call you, but I simply couldn't wait any longer to tell you that the experiment you suggested actually worked.' She had asked for a dream in spite of her doubts and was genuinely surprised when she awakened in the early hours of the morning with the vivid memory of a dream for the very first time in her life. She quickly added that it had not been a very long dream and was so silly that she was sure I could not extract any meaning from it. But at least she had remembered it!

There are many different types of dreams. There is a broad division between objective and subjective dreams: the former are usually experienced by people who are psychic; they are probably aware of this fact and know that they sometimes dream about actual events involving real people. These dreams have a distinctive flavour, or feeling, to them that is familiar to the dreamer. They rarely need to be decoded for they are usually only too clear, especially when the events in the dream actually come to pass.

I will, therefore, discuss only subjective dreams and their messages, for they contain the possibility of helping the dreamer in some way. Many people tell me that they often dream about a person or occasion that seems to have been triggered by a recent event in their life. This is frequently the case since the subconscious uses actual experiences and weaves them into a tapestry to portray a message it wishes to bring to the attention of the dreamer. Most people discover, often to their surprise, that as soon as they start to pay attention to their dreams they are given instructions on how to proceed in many areas of their lives. Dreams can be especially helpful in enabling people to recognise and accept the many varied aspects of themselves, some of which may be unconscious.

Our essential nature is of God, but our personalities are ego-created. This hides from us that our identity is divine, and keeps us enslaved by ego-power. We are not journeying to a remote and unattainable divinity. We need only to remove the coverings that obscure it from consciousness. That entails stripping ourselves of all our foibles, deceits, misconceptions, fears, prejudices and all the host of ego-related falsities, and it means consenting to be who we really are. Everything we are and everything we ever will be is already within us. But, until we know this and become fully conscious of all the overlay, we cannot begin to remove any part of it.

Dreams can help us detect the unconscious aspects of our personalities. By identifying the traits of the people who appear in our dreams, we can catch sight of unconscious attitudes, actions, habits, emotions and thoughts which may not necessarily express our true selves. We all have unconscious tendencies. That, literally, means that we are completely unaware of them operating in us.

Dreams can bring them to our attention and help us to become fully conscious of them, for only then can we deal with them.

As I have pointed out earlier, the language of the subconscious is couched in pictures and symbols, so aptly expressed by the Chinese saying, 'A picture is worth a thousand words.' Many of the oldest written languages, such as Chinese, Japanese and Egyptian, among others, were composed of pictographs. They very simply and clearly depicted pictures to denote people and objects to present the desired message to the reader. Gradually, as they were inscribed more and more quickly, they became simplified, until the original pictures were scarcely discernible. However, so gradual was the process, that the simplified version was as easily understood as the original pictographs. It was not until much later in man's development that non-pictorial alphabets came into existence.

The subconscious part of the mind is the oldest and most primitive. So it stands to reason that it will react more quickly and with greater comprehension to the original pictorial method of communication. A picture, or symbol, contains a whole idea or concept, whereas words can often be most frustrating when they do not fully express the desired thought.

Because we need the co-operation of the subconscious mind if we hope to put any change or growth into effect in our lives, it is wise to use its language to communicate our wishes to it. In that way we can send it directions to help us to bring about the intended results. We can also begin to understand the messages it sends to us in dreams and thus maintain a continuous two-way communication with it. The subconscious mind is actually very simple but, at the same time, truly wise. It will sometimes test us with hints to determine if we are open to accepting a message before it gives us a complete one. I call such dreams teasers. It also tries to act on all the messages we are constantly sending it via our thoughts and feelings. However, we do not always send it simple, uncomplicated directions. That is partly due to muddled thinking and conflicting ideas and wishes, and partly because we may have become too cerebral and cut off from our feelings. It is the emotional energy that carries a strong enough message to the subconscious to enable it to act on it. So, feelings reach it faster and more precisely than thoughts or words.

When endeavouring to interpret the messages in our dreams, we need to develop and use the functions of emotion and intuition rather than intellect and sensation. It is best to 'feel' into a dream, or comprehend its meaning in a flash of intuition.

With these guidelines in mind, we can be more successful in deciphering the messages our subconscious is trying to send us via dreams.

There are a multitude of symbols comprising the dream language. It is essential to know the meaning of those most likely to appear, if one is to understand the messages dreams contain.

Universal Symbols

Symbols can be general, that is universal in meaning, or personal. A universal symbol contains a message that has become associated with it for centuries all over the world, while the purely personal symbols stem from individual experiences. Both should be considered when seeking to unravel messages they may contain.

The universal or usually accepted meanings should be considered first, followed by the personal ones. Together they give the dreamer the keys to unlock the hidden meaning of the important messages he receives from his subconscious as it attempts to alert him to whatever he needs to know to rearrange his life more harmoniously.

Space is too limited to allow for this vast subject to be dealt with in any depth in this book. But, by giving the common derivations of some of the symbols most likely to occur in dreams, it is hoped that it might enable readers to start to unravel the meaning of their dreams. It can be a fascinating adventure.

First, the people who appear in dreams need to be examined. In the same way that real people can act as mirrors in which unconscious aspects of a person are reflected, the characters peopling dreams can also reflect facets of the dreamer. The action in the dream can be compared to a scene in a play depicting what takes place between the different characters, all living and acting out their needs, identities and desires within the person.

When a person is present as himself in a dream, the major part of his personality is represented. However, very few people always act, think, feel and speak as one whole, integrated person. Instead, it is as if a person is composed of a bundle of parts, like the cast of a play, each one portraying a separate role. Sometimes, their interaction is harmonious, but often the various parts are at variance with one another. Dreams can reflect this activity between the varying parts of a personality so that the person can become conscious of the need to bring them together into a more balanced whole.

All the masculine, or yang, parts can eventually be merged together into one main male figure and all the feminine, or yin, parts into one female figure, as the person works with his dreams. These two parts can then unite in an inner symbolic marriage, blending together the yin and yang: heart and head, or feeling and intuition with intellect and sensation. The result of this inner union will be shown in a dream as a gifted child who will develop into a newly balanced personality, fully conscious and capable of receiving the powerful energy of the High C when the time arrives to merge into it.

So, every character in a dream can be observed as representative of a part of the dreamer. Some are major parts while others may be quite small ones.

When recognisable people appear in dreams, some may be friends, and others not. To understand what they represent, it is helpful to jot down, as soon as possible after awakening, everything that comes to mind describing each person. When the various attributes have been outlined, the action in the dream needs to be studied to determine how these diverse facets are interacting within the person.

Supposing a person identifies a character attacking him in a dream as selfish. He can safely assume that a very selfish part of himself is undermining his principal self and that he is selfish despite the fact that he may not want to be and does not approve of selfishness.

Children and babies in dreams may symbolise either recently developing attributes, or facets of the dreamer still at the age level of the child and that need to be salvaged. For that reason, it is important to determine the age of the child and then count back that number of years to discover what was taking place at that time in the dreamer's life and that has continued to exist for that number of years.

An alternative method is for the person to think back to when he was the same age as the child in the dream to see what happened to retard the growth of that aspect, quality, talent or aptitude the child represents which now needs to be tended, accepted and encouraged to develop and attain the same age as the dreamer.

It can then be blended into the overall personality and not erupt in a childish way at inconvenient times.

People with dark or shadowy countenances appearing in a dream frequently represent unconscious parts of the dreamer. They reveal positive as well as negative aspects that have been suppressed at some time and that are now ready to be salvaged. In the same way as with a recognisable part, if it is negative, the Figure Eight needs to be practised and the part detached by whatever method is supplied by the High C. If it is positive, it should be welcomed and encouraged to become part of the main personality. The High C can be asked to send the necessary energy to be directed to the suppressed part, to give it strength and courage to rise up from its hiding place in the subconscious and become part of the whole person.

Obviously, sick, crippled, frightened or otherwise disturbed characters in dreams need to be healed, comforted, reassured and loved. They, too, are parts of the dreamer and are, therefore, his responsibility. The High C can be requested to supply the necessary instructions for attending to these parts.

When someone known to the dreamer appears in a dream he usually represents a conscious aspect or facet of the dreamer, so it is necessary to determine what he is like or what the dreamer's impression of him is. A very helpful method is to write down a description of him, listing his habits, attitudes and both positive and negative attributes in the dreamer's opinion. The facet he represents can then easily be ascertained from his interaction with the other characters in the dream.

Many people are dismayed when they are presented with aspects of their personalities in this way, but they can usually see the effect these parts have in their lives, especially in their relationships.

If the part acted out in the dream has a negative influence, it needs to be put into the Figure Eight and the exercise practised for two weeks. Frequently, this is sufficient to gain a helpful perspective and reduce the facet's control or negative influence. However, as an added precaution, the two circles can be separated and the High C asked to indicate any further steps that should be taken to prevent its continued domination.

At the same time, it is essential to watch for the influence of this facet of the personality in daily life. Every time the newly recognised unwanted behaviour becomes evident, the Figure Eight should be practised to lessen its hold. Any further need for that particular attribute also needs to be released. This can best be accomplished by breathing in whatever the High C supplies when asked to replace it, as it is essential to fill the void left by the departure of each small fraction of the person and breathe out any attachment to it.

If the characters in the dream are not known to the dreamer, the qualities they symbolise should be assessed from the way they interact on the inner scene. It can be devastating to be made aware of our well-hidden faults. No one enjoys seeing their own blemishes. It is so much easier to observe and criticise weaknesses in others. But we are responsible only for our own lives and not for other people's. Their lives are their responsibility.

The faster we become willing to put our own house in order, the less we will be tempted to judge others. We can then be a living example and, by working on our own problems, we may also be given the opportunity to share our insights with others.

Animals

In addition to people, both wild and tame animals often appear in dreams. All animals symbolise instincts. These are innate aptitudes that do not have to be learned. Their function is to protect and help people to stay alive. Babies are born with the basic instincts they share with all other living creatures.

Animals often appear in fables, myths, nursery rhymes, children's games and old sayings, so these sources should be checked for possible significance. For instance, 'He is like a big frog in a small pond' describes a person who is important only in his own small domain but would be insignificant in a larger territory.

There is also the fable about the frog who so desperately wanted to be important that he huffed and puffed and bloated himself up to be bigger and bigger. Unfortunately, as is often the case with those who resemble this self-important frog, he blew so hard that he burst, a casualty to overweening pride.

Wild Animals

If the animals in a dream are wild, such as bears, elephants, lions and tigers, the dreamer must determine what they signify to him personally, as well as their generally accepted meaning. He is being shown that he has within him wild or untamed instincts.

Many people report being chased by a wild animal in a dream. This would mean that they are being terrorised by one of their own wild instincts, depending on the meaning attached to the animal in question. We all have wild instincts inherited from our evolutionary foundation in the animal nature. They cause problems only if they control or dominate us rather than the reverse.

Tame or Domestic Animals

If a dream contains domesticated animals such as cats, dogs, horses, caged birds, fish, rabbits, hamsters and other pets, they signify instincts that have been tamed and are under conscious control in the person's life.

Dogs and Cats

In the method I have been taught, dogs symbolise extroverted or outgoing tendencies, while cats indicate introverted or more private and withdrawn behaviour. Both roles are equally important in maintaining balance in the individual. But they should be under his conscious control so that the appropriate one can be assumed at will to fit the occasion, instead of one being used continuously to the exclusion of the other.

A more detailed description of these two roles can be found in *Cutting the Ties that Bind*.

If, in a dream, a dog is sick or dead, this would constitute a warning that the dreamer is too introspective and not sufficiently outgoing. When a sick or lost cat is seen in a dream, the person is being warned that he is too extroverted and needs to find time to dive within himself and be more contemplative.

If either a cat or a dog attacks the dreamer, he should search to detect how the designated part is attacking him and take the necessary steps to remedy the situation. This applies to attack by any animal.

Horses

A horse in a dream signifies one's personal and instinctive way through life. It is a most important symbol because our instincts are the very foundation on which our lives are built. We need to be in touch with them and understand their function so that they can protect us and carry us through life safely and successfully, just as a well-trained horse carries its rider over every kind of terrain, including the hurdles along the way.

It is advisable to train and guide our instincts to take care of us in every kind of situation. On the other hand, we should not allow them to run away with us. We must be in control of them.

If a horse in a dream is sick or injured, it means that something has happened to impair the function of an instinct. A very effective exercise would be to re-live the dream and attend to the needs of the horse by taking it to a vet, feeding it, talking to it, stroking it and making contact with it as if it were an actual living animal. Quite often that is all that is needed to encourage it to develop and serve its master. At the same time it is helpful to watch for signs in everyday life that may be indicating areas where the instincts are not being supportive.

Fish

Fish symbolise parts of a person that are active in the subconscious but have not as yet emerged into consciousness. As soon as they are placed in the other circle of the Figure Eight, they can usually be consciously detected as taking part in the life of their host. As soon as they are recognised and acknowledged as belonging to the person, he can decide if they are an asset or a problem and behave accordingly, using the appropriate techniques.

(Frogs and toads are amphibian. They symbolise, intermittently, conscious and unconscious parts of the dreamer).

Birds

Birds symbolise the spirit or a heightened consciousness which can, like a bird, soar to great heights, free from the fetters that constrict earth-bound creatures. A skylark is perhaps the best example of such joyful freedom. If there is a sick or dead bird in a dream, it can mean the death or weakening of an inspiration or aspiration. What elevating or inspirational idea or plan has sickened or died? What has turned the dreamer away from the High C and Its direction and towards attachment to material things or activities?

Specific kinds of birds have gathered their own meanings. A peacock has come to denote pride, as in, 'As proud as a peacock,' probably due to the way a peacock preens and displays its beautiful tail.

A dove has become synonymous with peace. But it can also be an indication that the person is moving into new territory after a period of insecurity, like the dove sent out by Noah from the ark, to determine if the flood had abated after a long journey 'at sea'.

A hummingbird in a dream portrays a part of the person that is restlessly darting from flower to flower, sipping the honey each contains, just as so many people go from group to group in search of spiritual nourishment.

Butterflies sometimes have a similar connotation. But they can also denote the emergence of the person from the caterpillar-stage, that of consuming everything the world has to offer, and of the chrysalis-stage of withdrawal from the outer world, sometimes referred to as 'the dark night of the soul', or 'the cloud of unknowing', where everything is in flux and nothing is secure. When the butterfly, or imago, emerges from retirement, free to fly, it points to a breakthrough at some level.

An eagle appearing in a dream signifies strong spiritual aspirations, as in Isaiah 40: 31, 'They that wait on the Lord shall renew their strength; they shall mount up with wings as eagles.'

Yin and Yang

All objects appearing in a dream can be divided into two main categories according to whether they are yin or yang, heart or head, female or male.

Symbols that represent the yang quality are shaped like the male sexual organ and are long, pointed, phallic in shape, and assertive or thrusting in action. Guns, sticks, rods, poles, daggers and swords are all yang symbols. They represent the thinking, active part of both sexes.

Those objects that are considered yin in quality are shaped like the female sexual organs and are bowl-shaped, containers or receptacles. They are receptive and accepting. They include bags and purses, urns, jars, vases and even caves. They are connected to the emotions or feeling nature of both men and women.

Common descriptions such as someone has a 'rapier-like mind', or 'is an old bag', are examples of yin and yang qualities. So, according to its shape, an object will refer to either the feelings or the intellect of the dreamer. The message can be gleaned by applying the meaning to the activity in the dream.

Many people report dreaming that they lost a bag, purse or case, indicating that their ability to feel and be receptive is lost. Others mention losing a cane, or gun, which means that their thinking and active ability has been lost. A gun may be fired at someone in a dream, showing that the mind is too aggressive in the dreamer's life.

Moving Vehicles, Transportation

A bicycle in a dream signifies the person's balanced individual routine way through life. The opposite pairs of functions, sensation and intellect and intuition and emotion, or the male and female qualities, are being balanced when the dreamer rides a bicycle.

A wheelchair indicates that the part of the person symbolised by whoever is in the wheelchair is in some way crippled and is dependent on the main part of the person symbolised by the one pushing it, because it cannot function adequately.

A car symbolises the mechanical way through life for either a man or a woman. It refers to the dreamer's work or individual career on a routine daily basis. So, a car to a doctor would mean his medical practice, to a salesman, the work of selling, to a mother, the daily task of caring for the house, bringing up the children, shopping and attending to all the other innumerable chores of a householder's life.

If a car is lost or damaged in a dream, it is necessary first to ascertain how that message can be applied to the dreamer's daily life. It can be a warning that his job might end, or that something is wrong in the way it is being done. As with all dreams, the real meaning lies within the dreamer, so it is wise to ask the High C to help to decipher the message.

A taxi, being a temporary conveyance, usually denotes an interim job or occupation. It is a transition, or bridge, to a new activity.

If someone else is driving a car in a dream, it indicates that the dreamer is not in charge, but is allowing another part of himself to steer his way through life. If a woman is the driver in a man's dream, he is being shown that he is using his lesser function of feeling instead of his primary function of thinking in his job. If a woman dreams that a man is in the driver's seat, she is allowing her intellect to drive her and overshadow her natural emotions. The main part of the personality should be in charge, for the job to be done well and in a balanced fashion.

Buses, trains, trams and all larger modes of public transportation in a dream denote one's way through life in the work group or work arena, such as the whole company in which one works, the school in which one teaches, or the hospital in which one practises medicine.

Aeroplanes are mechanical and man-made. They symbolise flights of fancy, aspirations, plans and dreams, ambitions and fantasies. However, a plane cannot be perpetually airborne or it runs out of fuel or energy, and crashes. For a plan to be executed in daily life, the plane must land. In other words, the dreamer must bring his aspirations down to earth from the abstract level of pure thought into actuality.

Ships and boats are yin, or feminine, and symbolise the feeling way through life or the emotional life of the person. Some people dream that their ship is beached and no longer seaworthy, or in dry dock awaiting repairs. This usually means that they are without a satisfactory emotional way through life, that they need to salvage and launch it as they would an actual ship or boat.

I am often led to take a person back into a dream and ask him to do whatever the High C indicates to put the ship back into working order. This inner activity can take several days, even weeks, but the resulting freedom, to begin to feel again, is well worth the effort.

A house signifies the entire life of a person, its rooms have meanings according to their use. Many people dream of a house which is not the house in which they now live. Others report dreaming of a house where they lived in childhood or, perhaps, of their grandparents' house. Such messages mean that the person is not fully living up to his own true potential. If he dreams of a house in which he lived as a child, he may be living as a child in some part of his present life, or still be functioning under the control of his parents. If he dreams that he lives in someone else's house, he is living as they do and is not expressing himself as he really is.

Hotels, motels and inns, since they are temporary shelters, usually indicate that a change is in process that will lead the dreamer to a new perception of himself. A later dream may show him moving to a new house and, therefore, to that heralded new phase of his life.

The various rooms of the house also carry important messages according to the use to which they are put in daily life. For example, the basement refers to the subconscious. It must, however, be remembered that it contains both junk and treasure, suppressed possibly in childhood.

It is often a great help to set a person to work on the house he has seen in a dream, setting it in order, cleaning or renovating it to indicate what he needs to do to express himself more fully.

Dreams of going to the bathroom are very common, whether the purpose is to bathe, shower, wash hands, or to use the lavatory to urinate or defecate. The former signifies outer cleansing and refers to the outer life of the person needing to be cleaned up in some way that he is to discover; the latter indicates a need for an inner cleaning out, an elimination of negative facets, emotions, or thoughts. Dreaming that one is constipated or not able to find a lavatory generally implies that the person is blocked and either unable or unwilling to practise self-observation in order to see what he needs to discard. This may entail letting go of bad habits, attitudes, or an unsuitable way of life. Only he and the High C really know, so it is up to him to find out by asking the High C for help.

Bodies of Water

An ocean in a dream symbolises the collective unconscious that contains everything that has ever happened to the human race. This remains intact in the individual memory, but it is relegated to the unconscious.

Smaller bodies of water, such as ponds, lakes, swimming pools or puddles, represent the personal unconscious, where all the memories of the individual lie submerged.

Rivers are usually equated with the river of life, so they indicate the way through life that one's destiny dictates.

Rain usually means a blessing, since it is essential for life and growth and can turn a desert into an oasis.

Thoroughfares

Motorways, highways, roads and footpaths featured in dreams all denote the personal way through life, the destined path.

Personal Dream Symbolism

In addition to the foregoing general, or universal, meanings of various symbols commonly seen in dreams, the dreamer's personal associations must be considered. It is only reasonable to assume that the subconscious would choose symbols that are familiar to the dreamer if it expects its messages to be understood.

When carefully questioned about the meanings of some of the contents of a dream, a person will often be surprised at the associations that enter his mind. Again, it must be understood that the keys with which to unlock the meaning of a dream lie within the dreamer. In order to be revealed, it merely needs to be brought up into the conscious mind by impersonal questions that are not loaded or stressed in any way by the questioner.

Finally, it is essential to bear in mind that there is actually no foolproof or consistently effective or correct method of analysing dreams. The interpretation does not conform to the rigidity of a set method. It should be a creative partnership between the dreamer and the analyst, or helper, preferably with both participants using the Triangle so that they may both be guided by the superior wisdom of the High C in the final interpretation. Excellent results can be obtained when the dreamer is gently led back into the dream, and the High C is asked to supply the meaning of the various sequences as well as the main lesson. Repeatedly consulting the High C in this way is the only really effective method because the High C alone possesses all the answers. So it is a matter of listening rather than thinking, and then watching for thoughts to arise when the High C has been asked for elucidation.

I always hesitate to give specific examples of people's dreams and their interpretation because they are so very personal, applicable only to the dreamer. There is always the danger that other people may try to apply a particular interpretation to their own dreams, which may or may not be appropriate, since it would be out of context.

Another reason for my reluctance to be too specific is that it is essential for each person to work diligently to elicit the various messages or meaning from their own dreams, in much the same way as solving a crossword puzzle, cracking a code, wrestling with a Zen koan, or working on a jigsaw puzzle. The meaning of a dream always lies within the mind of the dreamer, so a facilitator should limit his help to supplying possible meanings to the various symbols, then plying the dreamer with questions to make it possible for the dreamer himself to extract the meaning of the dream sequence.

Chapter 31

THOUGHT
AND THOUGHT-FORMS

Since everything that has been created by man originated as a thought, a table, a house, a book, a painting, a symphony, a school and multitudes of other creations could not have been materialised unless someone first conceived each of them as an idea, a thought or a plan.

Thought is continually flowing in everyone in an unbroken stream, except when conscious thought is allayed during sleep and unconscious, or subliminal, thought takes over, often breaking through into consciousness as dreams. So, we are all continuously creating thought-forms, or sequences, with our thoughts, or repeating those thought-systems that we have acquired in childhood from our parents and other authority-figures.

To be manifested in a tangible form, abstract ideas and thoughts first have to be translated into words, energised by desire, or some other emotion, and then materialised by appropriate action, such as building a bridge, manufacturing an article, or writing a book. Many of our thoughts, hopes and plans are not invested with sufficient energy or enthusiasm to be brought into actuality. Both yin and yang energy are necessary for the creation of anything to take place. Yang is the moving, forming, projecting force, while yin is the receiving, incubating and nourishing one.

The more energy a thought is given, and the more frequently it is repeated, the more powerful and successful the eventual outcome. So, it is clear that we are always creating forms, either consciously or unconsciously, with our thoughts. We are, therefore, responsible for what we ourselves create with them, for they contain our energy which will return them to us in due course.

If we consider the theory of reincarnation and karma, it follows that we may have fashioned our thoughts into forms for many centuries and these too will return sooner or later, either to help or hinder us. It could also follow that our past thoughts have fashioned our present bodies, circumstances, relationships, joys and sorrows, the effects of which we may now be suffering or enjoying. Consequently, everything we are experiencing has been self-initiated, motivated according to our thought-processes and energised by our feelings.

We cannot erase the results of our past thoughts, but we can claim our birthright of free will. We can decide to use our thinking function positively in the present, and that will unfailingly affect the future. By reining in our runaway thoughts, we can nip in the bud any thought-forms that could result in a negative effect on our lives, and we can replace them with more positive ones more likely to produce beneficial results. In this way, we can gain some control over our lives and set in motion a more positive pattern for future incarnations.

Following on from the consideration of how individual thought can result in tangible forms, multiple thought-forms also need to be taken into account, for they, too, can have an influence on our lives.

A universal thought-form is a complex of many people's thoughts, beliefs and experiences on a specific subject over a long period of time. The more a thought is charged with emotion, the more powerful it becomes. So, when many people become attached to it and feed it with their energy, it increases even more.

All religious rituals, disciplines or bodies of information, commonly held beliefs, customs and mores, habits, superstitions, addictions and all the multitudes of multiple systems of thought that are accepted and added to by many individuals and groups are included in this category. Whatever we are attached to, either consciously or unconsciously, can link us to the powerful thought-forms governing the objects, habits or modes of behaviour we allow ourselves to be controlled by. A goal of accumulating enormous piles of money, or of attaining tremendous power, can also key us into the far more powerful forms controlling these activities.

One very interesting instance that illustrates the power wielded by thought-forms was brought to my attention just as this manuscript was ready to be typed.

Several young people, all approaching puberty, had asked to work with me at various times. After I had seen each of them, I noticed that they shared a common problem which manifested itself in fears and nightmares. Each of them had a current reason for fear, though not to the extent to which they were exhibiting it, so I suspected that a negative thought-form could be the cause. I secured their permission to check, by means of the reverie technique, to try to ascertain the underlying cause of their problem.

I was totally unprepared for the answer I received. I was shown that these young people had, through their own fears, linked up to a thought-form built around the ancient puberty rites handed down over the centuries by various national and tribal groups.

Many of these practices are very severe by our present standards. In primitive times, children who were nearing puberty needed to be carefully prepared to cope with all the different kinds of dangers which they might be likely to encounter when they became responsible men and women. Their livelihood would have to be wrested from an environment where they would be faced with wild animals, storms, members of other competing and unfriendly tribes and many other hazards. Necessarily, the trials they were forced to undergo needed to mimic the real-life dangers they would be most likely to confront. Many of these children were undoubtedly afraid, not only of the actual trials, but even more so of failing them. For, in that eventuality, they would have to continue to live in the group while being looked down on as failures, unworthy to participate in communal life as dependable adults.

Apparently, their fear was so intense that it was indelibly imprinted on the thought-forms that developed around the old rituals, which became more and more powerful as successive ceremonies added energy to them.

The young people I was seeing had keyed into these old masses of fear and their nightmares reflected the ancient rituals. Just having this explained to them helped them to understand, and knowing that the specific fears that had such a paralysing effect were destroyed was a great relief to all of them.

I was first introduced to the power that negative thought-forms can have on people's lives during our last visit to see Sathya Sai Baba. In the past, while at Baba's ashram in India, I have usually worked with those individuals who needed help. But, the last time there were far too many requests to fit into the time available during our two-week stay.

A friend who uses the work was also there at the time and had already worked with several people. I suggested that she and I set up the Triangle and work for, instead of directly with, those who were asking our help. In this way, we could look after many more requests in the limited time I was there. She was delighted at the suggestion and also hoped to be given insights into some of the more critical problems that had already been brought to her attention.

Over the years I have observed that there often appears to be a common theme to this work. I always refer to it as the theme of the week or month. A good illustration is the case of the two young women mentioned earlier, who came to work with me a day apart, both asking for help to overcome a very low self-image. Theirs was the request that elicited the technique of the Nest of Dolls.

I soon saw that the problems brought to us at the ashram this time also had a common theme. Most of these people said they felt as if they were under the influence of some kind of very powerful force from which they felt helpless to break free. What I did not at first realise was that these cases would thrust me into a new area of work dealing with problems rooted in a universal rather than a personal level.

I was shown that there are powerful and complex negative thought-forms, or patterns, active in the universe which control individuals if they tune into them through their own negative thinking, feeling or actions resonating on the same tone or wavelength. When such connections are made, often quite unconsciously, the thought-form, or archetype, being more powerful and complex, dominates them. Unfortunately, negative thought-forms are far more numerous than positive ones. As they proliferate and grow larger and more complex, with more and more people contributing to them, their control becomes even stronger and more widespread in its effect. It appears to be one of the chief causes of the troubled situation in the world today. We are, therefore, personally responsible for adding to their already powerful volume whenever we express negativity in any form. In addition, when people allow these thought-patterns to control them, they are directly contributing to the violence and corruption at present prevalent in the world.

These insights were revealed to me as we worked. I was reminded of the negative parental archetypes and the black clouds connected to certain families, nations, groups and places, both described earlier in this book and in more detail in *Cutting the Ties that Bind*. It was also reminiscent of the time when I was put in touch with a woman's dead artist husband who excitedly announced that he was now able to paint vivid pictures with thoughts and emotions instead of using paints and canvas, as he used to do when he was embodied. This too is described in my above-mentioned book.

Next, I was shown that by accepting the requests for help of the several people at the ashram, I would be led to the different multiple thought-forms controlling each of them and holding them helpless in their control. I began to understand why people who are addicted, compulsive, or obsessed find it so difficult, if not impossible, to break free. It is obvious that these thought-forms are more powerful than they are. This also explains why many addicts who seek professional help to break their particular addiction often, eventually, fall prey to other addictions, since they are not addressing the real cause, which may well be the powerful controlling thought-forms connected to the various addictions.

I must hasten to include a warning. I do not recommend this kind of work to be undertaken by those who are inexperienced with this method, or other similar ones, and especially if they are not in the habit of working under the guidance of the High C. Obviously, when dealing with such powerfully active forces there is a great danger of succumbing to their control or attack. Anyone dealing with them needs adequate protection to avoid such a hazard.

Each time I have been faced with such a task I have been shown how to protect both the person working with me on the Triangle as well as myself.

Since this phase of the work was started at Baba's ashram, we had the protection of his immense energy and love. However, even there, I was always guided to use specific protective devices to initiate a very necessary habit for future use.

Each time I asked within, from the High C, for insight into the people seeking help, I was guided to the overpowering force controlling them and shown how to destroy it and release the energy it contained for use in more constructive ways. Some of the patterns brought to my attention on the inner view were so bizarre that I began to wonder if I could either be imagining them or hallucinating.

At about that point in our stay, Baba called my husband and me to an interview. He immediately began to reassure me that he does work through me and speak through me, and that I must believe it and trust him and not fear that it was all due to my imagination. To our great amusement, he even mimicked my voice as he repeated what I often say, 'This is so crazy that I must be imagining it!' He continued to repeat variations on this theme each time he saw us, reassuring me over and over again that he is, indeed, helping and guiding me in the work and that I must believe it.

Since we returned home I have been overwhelmingly grateful for his repeated assurances. As I have continued to work, many of the problems brought to me have had their root cause in extremely powerful thought-complexes. Without Baba's assistance and persuasion, I am certain I would have panicked, concluding that I must be either crazy or guilty of indulging in the wildest fantasies.

The most exciting promise to emerge from this recent work is the prospect of helping to free the world from some of the powerful pockets of negativity that are controlling those who tune into them through their own negative thoughts.

Another insight I was given concerns the desecration and neglect of the earth and its environment. I was made aware of the urgent warnings now being given that it may even now be too late to rectify the situation we have ourselves brought about by our carelessness.

The earth is often referred to as Mother Earth. We are, finally, being forced to become aware that we have caused the present precarious imbalance by our lack of concern over our pollution of our planet's resources. It would appear that, in direct ratio to the way we have suppressed and scorned the feminine, or heart quality, in favour of the masculine, or head aspect, both in men as well as in women, so too have we neglected to revere the earth, our Great Cosmic Mother.

Now that women are beginning to demand the respect and acceptance rightfully due to them as the principal bearers of the nurturing function, we are all being made aware that this earth, upon which we live, is also in desperate need of help and care if it is to continue to support life. It cannot be taken for granted or ignored any more than the quality of femininity in any of its many forms can continue to be rejected.

We are being forced to rectify the heart bypass at the earth level as well as within each of us, to balance the head which has had the lead for far too long.

It would appear to be of no use merely to try to remedy the drastic situation solely on the concrete physical level, as so many of the recently formed ecology groups are trying to encourage people to do. Since everything tangible and visible in the world is the result of thought, which is invisible, there has to be a thought or idea before anything can be made manifest. The pockets of negative thought-forms are like cancer cells in the body of the earth, invisible, but becoming clearer as they increase. Therefore, the clean-up of the earth must take place simultaneously on the subtle level of thought-forms and on the gross material level for the healing of the earth to be accomplished. Otherwise, all the efforts to salvage our planet will have been in vain, for the negative thought-patterns will continue, unabated, to influence people and cause a resurgence of the very problems for which solutions are now being so desperately sought.

We are all responsible for saturating the ether with negative thoughts and feelings which have, over the centuries, produced the negative archetypes that are now so strong that they are controlling those of us who have contributed to their formation, resulting in a vicious circle.

Another major contributing factor, which adds to the growth of negative archetypes, is the concentrated violence, crime and unbridled negative emotions presented as entertainment on television and in films, magazines, books, newspapers and other forms of communication. Literally, masses of people are daily ingesting through their eyes and ears a tremendous amount of negativity which acts in much the same way as certain foods which, when taken into the body, poison or cause various illnesses. Baba says that food means anything taken in by a person through any of the five sense organs.

If we allow ourselves to absorb excessive amounts of negativity of any kind, we are deliberately inviting control by the negative archetypes.

If we hope to bring about a more peaceful world, with happier people inhabiting it, we must make a concerted effort to concentrate our thoughts on happier, more peaceful, loving, concerned and compassionate ideas, pictures and feelings. Let us feed the positive archetypes instead of the negative ones, which could be a way out of the present impasse. It is a challenge to each of us.

The next insight I was given was that the root cause of all the negative thought-forms spawned by people, eventually dominating them, is an alarming lack of love in our lives. This condition is so desperately painful and terrifying that many people turn away in anguish from facing it, and search instead for any means of escape from the torment of abject loneliness and hunger pangs of lovelessness.

This extreme and seemingly hopeless situation is the reason why Sathya Sai Baba has chosen to take human form at this particular time, just as other great teachers did in the past, whenever a similarly ominous situation had developed in the world. He is like a master generator who can recharge our weak batteries to enable us to reconnect ourselves to the High C.

We, with our limited strength, cannot change the critical situation facing the world. The powerful negative archetypes causing it require equally powerful positive ones to neutralise them.

But since we are all one at the High C level, when we tune into It and ask It to help us, we are automatically connected to Its vast network of energy and all the positive archetypes contained in it, which can have a strong positive impact.

So, let us start each day by asking the High C to think through us, feel through us, speak through us, act through us and, above all else, love through us. In that way we will be helping to disarm and destroy the awesome arsenal of ammunition composed of the accumulated negative thought-forms of multitudes of people for countless centuries which, like the hydrogen bomb, could easily eliminate us and the world in which we live.

We are given the gift of free will. That means, we are free to choose. So it is up to each of us to decide what we choose to do, either to add to the threatening disaster or to help to prevent it.

From my own observation over the past sixteen years, Baba presents a perfect role model to inspire us to follow his lead and apply his teachings to bring love back into the world to heal both the earth and ourselves.

INDEX

'always right' 107
ancient teachings   5, 68, 136,
    145, 152
animus and anima   117–19, 136
astrological charts   28–9

balloon 96–100, 112
beach ball 42–3
behaviour patterns 3, 5–6, 8,
    34, 47, 54–5, 67–8, 76, 91,
    104, 117
black cloud   10, 195

Ceiling on Desires programme
    17–18, 60
chakras   87
change   xii, 3, 5–6, 86, 109–10,
    152
choosing a midwife or
    doctor 22–3
clay models   124
Cosmic Parents   9, 39–41, 53,
    76, 98, 119–20, 128, 140, 144
crises   74
Cutting the Ties that Bind   4, 7,
    9–10, 36, 57, 67, 83, 98, 184,
    195
cutting ties   xiv, 6–7, 31, 41,
    49–50, 75–6, 81, 83, 90–1,
    93, 98, 127, 130, 132, 142–3,
    145–7, 174–5
cylinder   7, 43, 105

death experience   175
decision making   16, 34, 48, 72
dreams   76, 79, 100, 121, 128,
    155, 157, and ch. 20;
    animals in   183–6
    buildings and rooms in   188–9
    people in   180–3
    personal symbolism in 189–90
    recording   177
    thorough fares in   189
    vehicles in   187–8
    water in   189
    yin and yang   186–7

early influences   75–6, 81,
    99–105, 116
Edgar Cayce   154
education   xi, 3, 4, 19–20, 29,
    33, 44–5, 86
Education in Human Values
    programme   14, 33–4, 59

family heritage   3, 19, 23, 26,
    34, 54–5, 67, 72, 74–6, 80–1,
    89, 129
family relationships   9, 47, 54,
    91–5, 173
fifth aspect   44–5, 53
Figure Eight   7–9, 81, 83, 91,
    93, 99, 102–4, 107–8, 110,
    114, 117, 119, 121, 124, 127,
    134, 139, 143–6, 148, 182, 185

five tenets 14–17, 34
four functions 44–5, 47, 52, 87–8, 90, 179–80
free will 5, 8, 34, 40, 72, 81, 109, 152, 192, 198

God-force or source 13, 15, 67–8, 73, 77, 91, 112, 136–7, 143, 151, 168, 178
golden circle 7, 38, 43, 58–9,105

hall of mirrors 122–4
health 21
High C ix, xi, xii, xiii, xix, 5–6, 8–9, 15–16, 21, 31, 33, 35–7, 39–40, 47, 49, 53, 57, 64, 67, 69–73, 77, 80–2, 84, 86, 91–3, 98, 100–2, 105, 108–9, 116–17, 119–20, 122–5, 127–8, 130, 133, 138–41, 143–5, 147–8, 150–7, 161, 163, 165, 167–70, 172–4, 181–3, 185, 187–8, 190, 195, 198
Hitler 80, 131
hour glass 104–5

inner child 10, 123, 127–8, 149
inner house 9–10, 188
inner journey 68, 73, 109, 116, 130, 133, 140
instinct 34

jack 41–2, 138

karma 20, 68, 70, 72, 77, 81–3, 92, 109, 116, 152, 154, 172, 192

love xii, 12–13, 16, 34–5, 37, 40, 61, 87, 198 and ch. 10

mandala 45–6, 53, 87
mantra 14, 16, 72
masculinity and femininity 32, 84, 87–91, 119, 181
mass hypnosis 79–80
maypole 37–8, 57
media violence 61–2, 197

motives for having children 19–20

naming a child 25–7
nationality 88–9, 129, 131–3
negativity 4, 6, 9–10, 14, 20–1, 48, 50, 55, 67, 71, 117, 133, 194
neon blue light 7–8, 38–9, 81, 102, 108, 121
nest of dolls 100–4, 194
nightmares 42, 193

parents and authority figures xiv, 3, 5–8, 10, 11, 14, 19–20, 23, 25–7, 30–6, 39–40, 49–50, 54, 56, 62, 67–8, 71, 75–6, 79, 86, 91, 93–4, 97, 103–4, 191
past life recall 154–7, and ch. 29;
    Japanese girl 160–5
    Jew 165–6
    lessons from 174
    Lextra 171–2
    life at the time of Jesus 169–71
    Tibetan 166–7
'people pleaser' 97, 106
planet earth 17, 196–7
possessions and attachments 16, 21, 56, 68, 77–8, 82, 133–4, 151, 175, 185, 192
prejudice 131–2
preparing for the birth of a child 20–2
puppeteer and puppet 70–2, 117
pyramid 46, 53

qualities to be developed 69–70

reasons for, and purpose of, this life 30, 68, 78, 84–5, 116, 133, 151–4, 156
reincarnation 72, 76–7, 92, 133, 135, 150, 154, 192
'rejected child' 106
religions 34, 116, 129, ch. 27, 168;

Catholicism 138–42
Christian science 145–6
Christianity 137
Communism 148–9
Inquisition 138
Judaism 144–5
Mormonism 146–7
Protestantism 142–4
retrieving energy 83, 99–100, 108, 121, 124–5, 141
rituals and rites 8, 14, 24–5, 36, 49–50, 92, 129
role playing 13, 70, 83–4, 86, 88, 96, 104, 106–7, 109–11, 113, 117–20, 156

Sathya Sai Baba x–xiii, xiv, 12–14, 17, 20, 29, 33–4, 37–8, 51, 56, 60, 67–70, 92, 110, 112, 143, 167, 172, 194–8
scales and signposts 43–4
service 60, 115
sex 51–2, 156, 173
silent sitting 59
sin 137
soul mate 152

swastika 80
symbols 37, 79–81, 83, 91–2, 99–105, 108–10, 122–5, 127–8, 143–8, 179–90

thought-forms and archetypes 63–4, 79–81, 89, 98, 108, 150–1, 167 and ch. 31
transference 120–1
tree 9, 40, 53, 98, 119, 128, 140, 144
triangle ix, 39–40, 105, 109, 124, 127, 143, 147, 161, 190, 194–5
true self, teacher or guide xiii, xiv, 29, 31, 35, 44, 46, 55–6, 59, 67–8, 72, 84–5, 100, 112, 151–3, 156, 161, 178

unresolved problems 4, 61–4, 152

work as worship 13, 173

yin and yang 87, 90–1, 119, 186, 188

Phyllis Krystal is a psychotherapist of the Jung and Erickson schools. She was born in England but lives and works in California where she has developed her own techniques of psychotherapy. For over thirty years, she has been developing a counseling method using symbols and visualization techniques that help people detach from external authority figures and patterns in order to rely on their own Higher Consciousness as guide and teacher. To teach the method, Krystal gives lectures and seminars in the U.S. and many other countries. She is a devotee of Sathya Sai Baba, a world teacher living in India whose teachings and personal influence have been an inspiration. She is the author of *Cutting the Ties that Bind, Sai Baba: The Ultimate Experience,* and *Taming Our Monkey Mind* (1994) also published by Weiser.

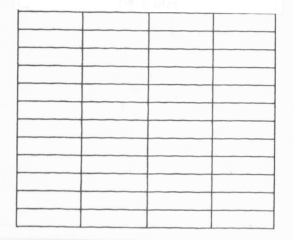